OXFORD

Biographies and Acknowledgements

Photographs by Chris Andrews

With grateful thanks to the University, Colleges and people of Oxford
who have so encouraged my photographic work.
Chris Andrews is Oxford's foremost artistic photographer. He began his career showing
photographs in the Summer Open Air Exhibition, Parks Road, Oxford, before going on to
publish a range of atmospheric cards, calendars and books, entitled 'The Romance of Oxford'.
Chris lives with his family in Oxford and his work covers areas from the Cotswolds and the
Chilterns to the Channel Islands.

For my parents, who enabled me to be an Oxford man, and for Jo always.
Author **Nick Hutchison** is a graduate of Worcester College, Oxford, where he read English.
He is a writer, actor and director, working in theatre, television and film; and has just finished
two years with the Royal Shakespeare Company. Nick also lectures on Shakespeare for the
Globe Theatre, frequently in Oxford. He lives in London and Suffolk.

All pictures courtesy of Chris Andrews except as follows:
The Bridgeman Art Library 197. All other photographs courtesy of the **Oxford Picture
Library**, photographs by **Chris Andrews** except: **Angus Palmer** pp. 25, 36, 57, 79, 81,
101, 107, 132, 134, 144, 168, 172, 173, 175, 179, 184, 188, 189, 190, 191, 192, 195. **Gareth
Jones** pp. 164, 46. **Suzie Barker** p. 51.

ISBN 0 75252 929 3

First published in 1999 by
SIENA
Queen Street House
4 - 5 Queen Street
Bath BA1 1HE

Copyright 1999 © Siena

This is a Siena Book

Produced for Siena by Foundry Design and Production,
Crabtree Hall, Crabtree Lane, Fulham, London SW6 6TY.

OXFORD

PHOTOGRAPHS BY
CHRIS ANDREWS

Chris Andrews

Text by Nick Hutchison

SIENA

Contents

Contents by Region

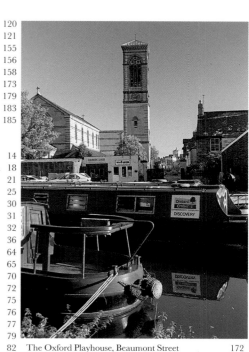

Introduction

*T*here is nothing in England to be matched with what lurks in the vapours of these meadows, and in the shadows of these spires – that mysterious, inalienable spirit, spirit of Oxford. Oxford! The very sight of the word printed, or sound of it spoken, is fraught for me with most actual magic.

Max Beerbohm, Zuleika Dobson

From the very first stirrings of learning in this foggy area of the Thames valley, by way of

Chaucer's Clerk of Oxenford, *and Max Beerbohm's*

Zuleika Dobson, *through to today's* Inspector Morse,

Oxford has always held a powerful grip on the minds and imaginations of the people of Britain, sustaining a reputation for academic excellence, eccentricity and architectural beauty unparalleled in these islands. The flapping of an academic gown behind an ancient bicycle; the early morning light glinting off the Radcliffe Camera's dome and turning sandstone walls to flame; the mist over Christ Church Meadows at dawn; May Day songs floating from Magdalen Tower; a punt floating lazily down the Cherwell – all these evoke the quintessential elements of Oxford. When Max Beerbohm celebrated the city so

fulsomely, he was merely affirming a widely-held belief about the special mystery that sets Oxford apart from other university towns, and particularly its great rival, Cambridge; 'the other place'.

Oxford holds an important position in every aspect of British life: no fewer than 25 British Prime Ministers are alumni of the University, including six of the last seven incumbents, and President Clinton, studied here, as did numerous other Heads of State and politicians. It has been a centre of religious thought and controversy throughout its tempestuous history; has held a position at the forefront of scientific progress and discovery, and has been a source of inspiration for many of the greatest artists, architects and writers that Britain has produced.

It is also a city of contrasts: being a busy industrial centre and county town as well as a centre of academic excellence, and the friction between 'town and gown' features largely in Oxford's history; a relationship that is sometimes amicable, sometimes aggressive, in the past sometimes even downright violent. It is this diversity of life that attracts tourists and residents

alike; some, like Anthony Wood, the famous seventeenth-century Oxford historian, reluctantly accept its dual nature: 'If you except the Colleges and Halls, the City of Oxford, in relation to buildings, is a very inconsiderable place, and no better than an ordinary Market Town'; others, such as

Nathaniel Hawthorne in 1856, actively dislike its variety: 'Oxford is an ugly town, of crooked and irregular streets . . . and as for the buildings of the University, they seem to be scattered at random, without any reference among one another.' In contrast, only 31 years later, the great guidebook writer Karl Baedeker wrote: 'Oxford is on the whole more attractive than Cambridge to the ordinary visitor, and the traveller is therefore recommended to visit Cambridge first . . . or omit it altogether.'

Today's visitor to Oxford cannot fail to be moved by the weight of history behind every wall and in every courtyard and quadrangle, for there is no part of Britain's turbulent past that is not etched in to some part of the city's fabric; no struggle or achievement in its history has failed to leave its impression on Oxford.

Oxford's origins lie in the late ninth and early tenth centuries, on the borders of two powerful kingdoms, Mercia and Wessex. It was, as its name suggests, built on the site of an old ford for oxen across the Thames, a causeway probably constructed in the late eighth century. According to tradition, a refugee Mercian princess, Frideswide, founded a religious community of women here in the eighth century, later becoming patron saint of the city, beginning Oxford's long association with matters of religion. The town grew rapidly throughout the Middle Ages, largely because of its position at the centre of the north–south and east–west trading routes and, although the Norman Conquest destroyed many of

the buildings, by the twelfth century it had revived sufficiently for Henry I to visit and stay at a royal residence called Beaumont, near to where Worcester College now stands.

Although many medieval writers claimed that the University started in the early Dark Ages, some naming King Alfred as its founder, others asserting more wildly that it dated back to the time of Christ, it is certain that by the end of the twelfth century Oxford had already acquired its reputation for learning. In c. 1190, a prior of Worcester said the town was 'abounding in men skilled in mystic eloquence, weighing the words of the law, bringing forth from their treasures things new and old,' and the first recorded Master of Arts of the University, Edmund of Abingdon, who died in 1240, laid down a precept to his pupils which still rings true today: 'Study as if you were to live forever; live as if you were to die tomorrow'.

By the thirteenth century the College system had begun in the University, and in 1410 it was decreed that all students must live in recognised halls of residence; the basis of student life that continues

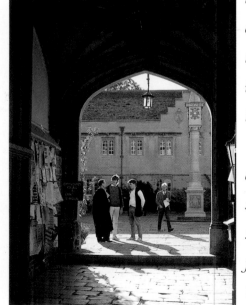

to the present day had been established, whereby a student is attached to a specific College rather than the University as a whole. Chaucer's clerk in 1400 would surely have recognised the lifestyle of his twentieth-century counterpart.

In the centuries that followed the fortunes of the town and the University fluctuated dramatically; Henry VIII founded Christ Church College in 1532, and Elizabeth I visited on several occasions and was much pleased with her reception from the University. A Royalist stronghold during the English Civil War, it was used by King Charles I as his headquarters for four years from 1642, but eventually was forced to surrender to the Parliamentarians, and the University was badly damaged. As Anthony Wood wrote, 'there was scarce the face of an

University left, all things being out of order and disturbed'. The Restoration saw renewed prosperity for both city and University, and indeed, gave it enough power and influence to withstand the might of the king, when in 1687, James II attempted to force the colleges to accept Catholicism.

After such turbulent times, the University settled down to a period of indulgence; in the eighteenth century it was labelled by one observer as a centre of 'port and prejudice', but the more rigorous approach to scholasticism and religion that

prevailed in the nineteenth century allowed the University to expand and to extend its predominance in every area of British society, putting it at the centre of our cultural, scientific and political life, whilst at the same time retaining the academic independence for which it is famous.

It is a University that can accommodate Cardinal Newman and Oscar Wilde; Lawrence of Arabia and William Morris; John Wesley and Beau Brummel; that taught both Gerard Manley Hopkins and John Betjeman; and that celebrates the Classical architecture of Christopher Wren, the Victorian Gothic of Keble College and the stark Modernism of St Catherine's. Above all, it is a place where the past and the present coexist in perfect harmony in an atmosphere of learning; Matthew Arnold wrote in 1865, 'and yet, steeped in sentiment as she lies, spreading her gardens to the moonlight, and whispering from her towers the last

enchantments of the Middle Age, who will deny that Oxford, by her ineffable charm, keeps calling us ever nearer to the true goal of all of us, to the ideal, to perfection – to beauty in a word, which is only truth seen from another side . . . Adorable dreamer, whose heart has been so romantic! who hast given thyself so prodigally, given thyself to sides and heroes not mine, only never to the Philistines!'

DREAMING SPIRES

*The view across the rooftops of Oxford is the most famous,
and the most magical, that the city has to offer. The spires have proved the
inspiration for hundreds of writers, poets and artists over the centuries.*

Autumn View
SOUTH PARKS

Oxford, the city of dreaming spires, has attracted generations of visitors from its very early days as a University; always amongst these have been some of the greatest writers of the time. Possibly more poetry and prose has been written celebrating Oxford than any other town or city in the United Kingdom, and this magical place has inspired writers to some of their finest works.

One of the main sources of inspiration has always been the view of the Oxford skyline from a distance, with its magnificent array of towers, spires and domes catching the sun, or veiled in the morning mist that rolls in from the Rivers Cherwell and Isis (the Oxford name for the stretch of the Thames that flows through the city). Seen here, bathed in autumn sunlight, are some of the most familiar of those landmarks: the spire of St Mary's; the University Church; the

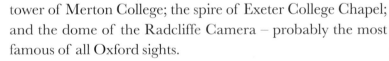

tower of Merton College; the spire of Exeter College Chapel; and the dome of the Radcliffe Camera – probably the most famous of all Oxford sights.

Across The Isis
CHRIST CHURCH MEADOW

The phrase 'dreaming spires' comes from the poem 'Thyrsis', by Matthew Arnold – one of Oxford's most famous sons. A student at Balliol, he returned as a fellow of Oriel College in 1845 and was elected Professor of Poetry in 1857. As well as coining the phrase 'dreaming spires', Arnold was also the author of another of the most famous epithets about Oxford: 'the home of lost causes', and it is the intellectual and philosophical variety of Oxford that has appealed to so many great thinkers over the centuries.

The lines from Arnold's poem describe the view of Oxford on a winter's evening – albeit a warmer one than that pictured here, with the frost thick on Christ Church Meadow behind the chilly Isis:

This winter-eve is warm,
Humid the air! leafless, yet soft as Spring,
The tender purple spray on copse and briers!
And that sweet city with her dreaming spires,
She needs not June for beauty's heightening.
Lovely all times she lies, lovely tonight!-

WINTER SUNRISE
CENTRAL OXFORD

Oxford's capacity to inspire is not limited to poets and writers; it has touched many of the greatest visitors to the city. Anthony Wood, the celebrated seventeenth-century Oxford historian, recounts in his history of the city a visit by Queen Elizabeth I. As she was leaving Oxford, she was escorted by all the Clerks to the eastern edge of the city; here the Queen thanked the Chancellor for his hospitality, 'and then looking wistfully towards Oxford said to this effect in the Latin tongue "Farewell, farewell, dear Oxford, God bless thee and increase thy sons in number, holiness and virtue." and so went towards Ricote.' It is typical of that most eminently practical of monarchs that her greatest desire was that the University should grow in size and, therefore wealth.

Royal patronage has not always been so kind to the city: Charles I's residence here during the Civil War led to a long and bitter siege; however, perhaps mindful of past favours, Oxford remained staunchly Royalist.

Summer View
SOUTH PARKS

Just as Royalty has been impressed by the breathtaking beauty of the Oxford skyline, so too have more prosaic writers. In 1578 Ralph Aga, a cartographer, produced the first accurate map of the city, showing it from a northern perspective, as pictured here, and although not a poet, he felt moved to write as an introduction to the work:

The measure form and sight I bring
Of ancient Oxford, nobleness of skill
A city seated rich in everything,
Girt with woods and water, pasture, corn and hill.

One hundred and fifty years later, in 1707, the same view of the city inspired the poet Thomas Tickell to write his poem 'Oxford':

For wheresoe'er I turn my wond'ring eyes,
Aspiring tow'rs and verdant Groves arise,
Immortal Greens the smiling Plains array,
And mazy Rivers murmur all the way.

It is a tribute to the enduring magic of Oxford that, despite its growth as a commercial and industrial centre throughout the twentieth century, its power to inspire remains undiminished, and the magnificent views it affords are untouched by the march of progress.

St Mary's Church & The Radcliffe Camera
CENTRAL OXFORD

By the nineteenth century, the famous skyline that can be seen today was all but established and most of the best-known landmarks had been constructed. It was at this time that much of the best writing about Oxford was published. Thomas Hardy set his novel *Jude the Obscure* in and around Oxford, calling it Christminster. He describes the impression the city makes on his hero when seeing it for the first time: 'Some way within the limits of the stretch of landscape, points of light like topaz gleamed.

The air increased in transparency with the lapse of minutes, till the topaz points showed themselves to be the vanes, windows, wet roof slates, and other shining spots upon the spires, domes, freestone-work, and varied outlines that were faintly revealed. It was Christminster, unquestionably; either directly seen, or miraged in the peculiar atmosphere.'

Although Hardy found the University a discouraging, elitist place in the novel, there is no denying the powerful draw it exerts on his hero; Jude is entranced by the city just as he is destroyed by it.

Oxford Skyline
NEW COLLEGE

It was the Romantic Movement that truly took Oxford to its heart; John Keats wrote home in a letter in 1817: 'This Oxford I have no doubt is the finest city in the World – it is full of old Gothic buildings – spires – towers – Quadrangles – Cloisters – Groves &c and is surrounded with more clear streams than I ever saw together. I take a walk by the side of one of them every evening and thank God.'

Three years later, William Wordsworth, although a graduate of 'the other place', Cambridge, felt moved to write:

Yet, O ye spires of Oxford! domes and towers!
Gardens and groves! your presence over-powers
The soberness of reason; till, in sooth
Transformed, and rushing on a bold exchange,
I slight my own beloved Cam, to range
Where silver Isis leads my stripling feet,
Pace the long avenue, or glide adown
The stream-like windings of that glorious street –
An eager novice robed in fluttering gown!

Such sentiments may have been shared by many Oxford graduates, but cannot have won him many friends in his own University.

The Spires
THE PARKS

The mystery of Oxford appealed strongly to the aesthetic minds at the University. Edward Burne-Jones, the Pre-Raphaelite, wrote in 1853: 'Oxford is a glorious place; godlike! at night I have walked around the colleges under the full moon, and thought it would be heaven to live and die here.'

The most famous aesthete of them all, Oscar Wilde, was a student at Magdalen College. Oxford exerted a great influence over his imagination – just as it had over many other writers, both before and since – causing him to pen his poem 'The Burden of Itys' in praise of the city:

And far away across the lengthening wold
Across the willowy flats and thickets brown,
Magdalen's tall tower tipped with tremulous gold
Marks the long High Street of the little town,
And warns me to return: I must not wait.
Hark! 'tis the curfew booming from the bell in Christ Church Gate.

There can be little doubt, even in today's more cynical climate where students change Arnold's dreaming spires into the 'city of perspiring dreams', that Oxford still has the power to move and to inspire, and that it retains both its magic and its mystery still.

ACADEMIC & RELIGIOUS OXFORD

*Born of both academic and religious ideals, many buildungs in Oxford
epitomise the city's origins and ethos. Churches, libraries and Examination Schools
each have their chapter in Oxford's story, past and present.*

The University's Heart
CENTRAL OXFORD

Seen from above, with the roofs catching the sun and the spires and domes casting their morning shadows, this is the heart of the University. Bounded by the High Street to the south and Broad Street to the north, this is the very centre of academic life in Oxford, with the familiar round form of the Radcliffe Camera at its mid-point. The spire of St Mary's, the University church; the pinnacles of All Souls; Exeter and Lincoln College chapels; and the flash of white that is the cupola of the Sheldonian Theatre can all be seen here – some of the University's most important landmarks.

Oxford University has no official centre, just as it is not a single academic establishment. The collegiate system, which had been established

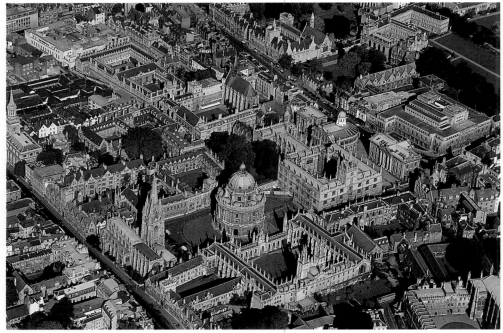

by the thirteenth century, means that any student or don is attached to a specific college. Although these colleges are in turn attached to the University, they retain, in many cases, a very individual identity. However, the sense of being an 'Oxford man' is strong; Baron Coleridge wrote in the mid-nineteenth century: 'I speak not of this college or of that, but of the University as a whole; and gentlemen, what a whole Oxford is!'

The Martyrs' Memorial
ST GILES

Standing at the southern end of St Giles, the Martyrs' Memorial is a testament to Oxford's troubled religious past. Built in 1841, and designed by George Gilbert Scott, it is based on the thirteenth-century Eleanor Cross at Waltham in Essex. It commemorates the execution of three Anglican bishops – Ridley, Latimer and Cranmer – during the reign of the Catholic Mary Tudor, 'Bloody Mary'.

These three unfortunates were examined for their Protestant beliefs in the Divinity Schools, before being sentenced to death by burning at the stake. Ridley and Latimer were killed first, on 16 October 1555; Cranmer had to wait for papal sanction. During that time he recanted his beliefs, but was sentenced to death anyway. Tradition has it that he thrust the hand that had written his recantation into the fire first. It is Latimer's final words, however, that have taken their place in history: 'Be of good comfort, Master Ridley, and play the man. We shall this day light such a candle, by God's grace, in England, as I trust shall never be put out.'

Merton Library
MERTON COLLEGE

One of the first Colleges at Oxford, founded in the thirteenth century, Merton was also one of the first to boast a library, a rarity in times when books were extremely expensive and difficult to come by. The first printing did not take place in Oxford until about 1478, so Merton's original manuscripts would all have been hand-written and bound, many with beautiful and intricate illuminations.

A record of the first 12 books acquired by the College show how heavily University learning concentrated on the philosophy of religion; it includes only one secular work, *De Animalibus* by Aristotle. All the others were either religious texts, such as 'half the Psalter, glossed', or commentaries on such texts. By 1360, the theological manuscripts alone were valued at £132 (this was about half the worth of a ship in the Navy at the time) so Merton's dons had every reason to be proud of their library, and they took great care of their books, keeping them chained, just as they are here.

Bulldogs
CHRIST CHURCH COLLEGE

As the University expanded, it became clear that some form of restraining laws had to be laid on the students, and that such laws had to be enforced. The University therefore instituted the office of Proctors, first mentioned in documents dating from 1248. The Proctors are elected from the various colleges in rotation, and have disciplinary authority over all students at the University, whatever their college.

They are accompanied on their patrols by 'bulldogs' – University policemen instantly recognisable by their bowler hats. It is their job to recognise the students or members, and in the nineteenth century they were also expected to distinguish between a respectable female and a 'character' – a woman of ill-repute. The bulldogs are legendary for taking their responsibilities very seriously; James Woodforde, a Proctor at the time, writing in his diary of 1774, describes arresting a student called Hawkins for 'carousing with low-life people': 'he was terribly frightened and cried all the way to his college, and was upon his knees very often in the street, and bareheaded all the way.' Hawkins probably had his reasons; often the punishment for such a crime was being sent down (expelled).

The Oxford Union
ST MICHAEL'S STREET

Possibly the most famous debating society in the world, the Union was founded in 1825, and originally held its meetings in rented rooms in the High Street. In 1855 the society bought these new premises in St Michael's Street. A new debating chamber was built, designed by Benjamin Woodward of Dublin (also responsible for the University Museum) and, although this chamber was replaced in 1878 with a larger one, and is now the Union library, it was a source of inspiration to the Pre-Raphaelite painters William Morris and Edward Burne-Jones, who decorated it with Arthurian scenes in the summer of 1857. Sadly, their youthful enthusiasm did not extend to preparing the walls adequately, and their efforts have long since disappeared, although Morris later returned to paint the vaulted roof.

The Union has been the scene of many famous debates, most notably in 1933 when a motion 'This House will in no circumstances fight for its King and Country' was passed by 275 votes to 153, causing a national scandal, and convincing many of Oxford's moral decadence.

The University Museum
PARKS ROAD

The University Museum in Parks Road is eloquent testimony to Oxford's place at the heart of both scientific and architectural debate, and the storm clouds glowering above it here mirror perfectly the controversy it caused.

The sciences had always been considered poor relations of the classics and theology, but in the mid-nineteenth century many eminent scholars began to argue a proper place for them at the University, as well as a decent building to house the faculty. Among the champions of this cause were John Ruskin, a noted Oxford scientist, and Henry Acland, the man most influential in the creation of the Museum. In 1855, work began on the new building, designed by architect Benjamin Woodward, and built in the new Continental Gothic style which so divided critics of the time.

In 1859, Ruskin wrote of the finished building, 'now therefore, and now only, it seems to me, the University has become complete in her function as a teacher to the youth of this nation'. Alfred, Lord Tennyson was less flattering; walking past the Museum in 1860 he merely remarked: 'perfectly indecent'.

University Museum Interior
PARKS ROAD

The inside of the Museum was no less controversial than the Gothic exterior, not only for its design, but also for what it contained. The offices, laboratories and lecture rooms surround a large, glass-roofed courtyard, constructed in an Italian style by Francis Skidmore from wrought iron and glass supported by Gothic columns. It is this courtyard that houses the exhibits, including the dinosaur skeletons and the famous dodo skeleton which first came to Oxford in 1683 as part of John Tradescant's collection.

The Museum was the setting for many debates in the nineteenth century, as arguments raged about Darwin's theories of evolution. The most famous of these occurred only a year after the building was completed, in 1860. In an acrimonious debate, the Bishop of Oxford concluded his venomous attack on the evolutionists, specifically Thomas Huxley, by asking which side of his family was descended from apes. Huxley famously replied that he was not ashamed to have a monkey as his ancestor, but that he would be ashamed to be connected with a man who used his great gifts to obscure the truth. The evolutionists won the day.

The Radcliffe Observatory
GREEN COLLEGE

O ne of many bequests to the city of Oxford from the estate of John Radcliffe (the physician to Queen Anne, whose legacy to the University is unparalleled), the Radcliffe Observatory was built at the instigation of Thomas Hornsby, the Savilian Professor of Astronomy. Begun in 1773, but not completed until 1794, it was primarily the work of James Wyatt, who was to become one of Oxford's most important architects. Built in the Neo-Classical style, it is inspired by the Tower of the Winds in Athens, and is sometimes known by that name. The large windows at the top are designed for the use of telescopes, and it has a lecture room on the ground floor. The whole building is a testament to the increasing importance of science within the University that was to reach its zenith in the mid-nineteenth century.

It was Hornsby who suggested that the Observatory should have a full-time, salaried keeper; among those who held this position over the years was the Oxford eccentric, Professor Robertson, who instructed his housekeeper, just before his death, 'how to treat his corpse, tie up his chin, to lay him out etc.'.

Oxford University Press
WALTON STREET

The history of printing in Oxford goes back to the fifteenth century and, like so many of Oxford's institutions, there is some controversy as to its precise origins. It would appear that Oxford's first book was published by Theodric Rood in 1478, from his press in the High Street. By the time the Sheldonian Theatre was completed in 1669, the University had its own press, which Wren's designs had to incorporate. The press moved to the Clarendon building opposite in the eighteenth century, but at the beginning of the nineteenth century, with the demand for books growing rapidly, it became clear that larger premises were required.

Accordingly, the present University Press was built in the north-west of the city, on Walton Street, a massive Classical edifice designed along Roman lines by Daniel Robertson. Today the OUP is one of the world's most renowned academic publishers, producing many important volumes every year, although the underlying philosophy, satirised in the Oxford Magazine of 1892, still applies:

Some books were to stimulate learning,
And some were intended to sell.

All Souls Chapel
HIGH STREET

Uniquely among the Oxford colleges, All Souls College is not open to undergraduates; it boasts the intellectual élite of the University, and to become a fellow of the college is one of the highest academic honours in Britain. Founded in 1438 by Henry Chichele, Archbishop of Canterbury, it was established as a place for training the clergy and church lawyers, and the magnificent chapel demonstrates this emphasis on religion. The marvellous stained glass and the hammerbeam roof in the chancel are both original, and although the chapel underwent much revision, overseen by Wren in the seventeenth century, later restoration has returned it to its fifteenth-century grandeur.

In this chapel the fellows were required to pray for the souls of all those who had died penitent, but particularly the victims of Henry V's wars in France, and the college still possesses the original statues of both King and Archbishop dating from its foundation. It is easy to see why Henry James, writing in 1905, described the fellows of All Souls as 'having no obligation save toward their own culture, no care save for fine learning as learning and truth as truth, [they] are presumably the happiest people in the world'.

Trinity College Chapel
BROAD STREET

One of the most beautiful of all the Oxford chapels, Trinity represents the high point of late-seventeenth century church architecture, although ironically its architect remains anonymous. Frequently attributed to Wren, he actually only became involved after building work had begun; the original designer of this Baroque masterpiece is unknown.

The chapel was founded by the College President, Ralph Bathurst, in 1691, after the previous chapel had fallen into disrepair, and the work was completed in 1694. The woodwork and plasterwork of the interior are quite exquisite; the juniper wood screen and reredos are surmounted with reclining figures, and over the altar there are delicate carvings, including a sunburst representing the Deity. Once again, it is not known for certain who the craftsman was, although it is possible that Grinling Gibbons, the greatest wood-carver of the century, was responsible. Whoever the mysterious artisans who conceived and constructed this beautiful place, it remains one of the most inspiring of all Oxford's religious buildings.

The Ashmolean Museum
BEAUMONT STREET

There has been an Ashmolean Museum in Oxford since 1683 when Oxford antiquary, Elias Ashmole opened his new museum in premises on Broad Street. The idea was primarily to allow the public access to the collection of rarities brought back to England by the two John Tradescants, the sixteenth century traders and explorers. Among this collection, now in the University Museum, was the famous dodo skeleton, as well as objects of more questionable value: 'Item; divers things cut on plum-stones.'

The modern Ashmolean stands on the corner of Beaumont Street and St Giles, and was built between 1841 and 1845, originally to house the University's art collection, which had expanded beyond its home in the Bodleian Library. Designed by Charles

Cockerell to a Classical design, it is an extremely imposing building, standing high above street level, with two wings flanking a long gallery, and an ornate Greek portico facing Beaumont Street. Thanks to a long line of benefactors and donations, it has become one of the best art galleries of its size in the country, containing many fine collections of paintings, drawings and sculptures.

St Mary's Church
HIGH STREET

The religious centre of University life since the Middle Ages is St Mary's, or the University church which stands at the very heart of academic Oxford in the middle of the High Street, backing onto Radcliffe Square. Built sometime in the early fourteenth century, the oldest surviving part is the spire, one of the most spectacular features of the Oxford skyline.

From its very beginning this church was central to University life. An important forum for the clerks, it became the meeting place of the Convocation, or governing body, as early as the thirteenth century, and the Chancellor's Court, the disciplinary committee, also met here. By the fifteenth century the building had largely fallen into disrepair, and around 1462 the Bishop of Norwich, a former Provost of Oriel College, paid for the rebuilding of the chancel. The rest of the building was then gradually replaced – funded by public subscription and helped by a gift of timber from Henry VII – in the form that exists today, leaving only the spire as evidence of the earlier church.

Duke Humfrey's Library
OLD SCHOOLS QUAD

Now a part of the Bodleian Library, Duke Humfrey's Library predates its more famous successor by some 150 years. With the rapid spread of learning throughout Europe in the fifteenth century, the possession of manuscripts became a source of much pride and a means of attracting visiting scholars to the University. In 1444 Humfrey, Duke of Gloucester, younger son of Henry V and a renowned patron of classical learning, gave a large collection of books to the University. It was agreed that these must be housed in a library befitting their donor, and eventually it was decided that a special room would be built for them, above the newly-created Divinity Schools.

A shortage of funds prevented this happening for some 30 years: the University begged Parliament for the necessary money, without success. In the 1470s, a public subscription was launched, the largest donor being Thomas Kemp, Bishop of London, who gave 1,000 marks. Finally, in 1488, Duke Humfrey's Library was opened to readers, 40 years after his death; the cruellest indignity was that a large part of his private library, originally destined for Oxford, eventually ended up in Cambridge.

The Tower of the Five Orders
SCHOOLS QUADRANGLE

The tower of the new Schools Quadrangle, begun after Bodley's death, was completed in 1624, and is called the Tower of the Five Orders as each vertical section displays a different Classical order of columns, four of which can be seen here: Doric, Ionic, Corinthian and Composite.

The Tower's design was altered during its construction in 1620 to commemorate a visit to the University by James I, and the sculptural group in the centre depicts the King presenting his writings to the University, attended by Fame with a trumpet. The Royal Coat of Arms was also incorporated at the top of the Tower.

James was enormously impressed by the Bodleian, and remarked: 'If I were not a King I would be a University man; and if it were that I were a prisoner, if I might have my wish, I would have no other prison than this library, and be chained together with these good authors.'

The Bodleian Library
OLD SCHOOLS QUAD

Sir Thomas Bodley stands as the most significant benefactor in the University's history; a politician and scholar, and a fellow of Merton College, he was a man of considerable fortune, partly through marriage to a rich widow. In 1598, the state of the University Library had become appalling, and Bodley applied his wealth to restoring it to its former glory. Founded in 1598, the library opened to readers in 1602, using the existing Divinity Schools building, and restoring Duke Humfrey's library to its original state.

In 1610, however, an agreement was made with the Stationers' Company in London, stating that a copy of every book registered in Britain had to be placed in the Library (a statute which still holds true today), and it immediately became clear that expansion was necessary. Bodley yet again

dug deep into his own fortune to build an extension, and then even further in order to finance the building of the new Schools Quadrangle, which housed the University's lecture and examination rooms.

Bodley died before the project was completed and was buried in Merton, but his contemporaries knew that his legacy to the city would be a permanent memorial. The poet Henry Vaughan wrote:

Thou canst not dye! here thou art more safe
Where every Book is thy large Epitaph.

The Radcliffe Camera
RADCLIFFE SQUARE

The Radcliffe Camera is probably the best known and best loved of all Oxford's buildings, and is one of the finest Classical buildings in England. It stands at the very centre of the University and was built at the bequest of John Radcliffe, Queen Anne's physician, who left £40,000 for its construction; he stands with Bodley as one of the greatest benefactors of the University, and it is fitting that the former's greatest memorial should now be a part of the latter's.

Construction on the Camera did not begin until 1737, 23 years after Radcliffe's death, and the process was extremely slow as the architects had to wait for the site to become fully available. Begun by the celebrated architect Nicholas Hawksmoor, it was completed after his death by James Gibbs. Known originally as Radcliffe's Mausoleum, it became a part of the Bodleian Library in 1862, at which point the arches around the base were filled in to create an extra reading room, and the building gained its current name, the Radcliffe Camera.

Radcliffe Camera Dome
RADCLIFFE SQUARE

Like to a Queen in pride of place, she wears
The splendour of a crown in Radcliffe's dome.

Lionel Johnson

Seen here across the pinnacles of the Bodleian building, the Camera has been a central part of University life since its foundation in the eighteenth century, and is one of the University's most enduring symbols.

It was in the Camera in 1844 that the Duke of Wellington, then an old man, felt incapable of climbing to the top to escort the Prince of Prussia, remarking that 'this sight-seeing is damned tedious work'. In the nineteenth century, Lord Eldon found an elderly don, much the worse for drink, feeling his way home along the Camera's walls, and so going round and round in a perpetual circle. It was from the roof of the Camera, also in 1844, that a student supporter of the theologian John Henry Newman pelted the Vice-Chancellor of the University with a shower of snowballs to protest at the official condemnation of Newman's thesis 'Tract XC'; and it was from here that Thomas Macaulay looked down on 'the magnificent sea of turrets and battlements below'.

The Sheldonian Theatre Roof
BROAD STREET

The Sheldonian Theatre was built in 1664 as a ceremonial centre for the University, which had outgrown St Mary's Church (not least because some of the celebrations had become rather too indecorous for a religious setting). The idea of a new building came from the Dean of Christ Church, John Fell, and a site was bought north of the Divinity Schools; but it was the appointment of the young Christopher Wren as architect – then only 33 years old – that was the critical moment in the project. Although already recognised as a genius in many different areas of learning, this was Wren's first large building, and his achievement with it propelled him in to the front rank of architects.

The most difficult challenge was to erect a roof with a span much wider than anything that existed at the University, so that the audience could see and hear ceremonies clearly. Using a system of long beams, diagonal struts and vertical supports, Wren created the roof, and then had it disguised with the magnificent allegorical painting of Truth by the royal artist Robert Streater. The effect was considered a triumph, and the reputations of both Fell and Wren were guaranteed.

The Sheldonian Theatre
BROAD STREET

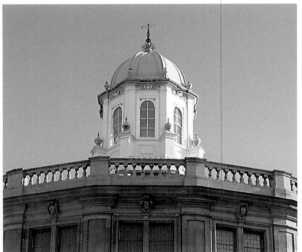

The original intention of the University authorities was to use the Sheldonian for dramatic performances, anatomical lectures and debates, as well as for the ceremonial needs of the University. This idea was dropped soon after Wren submitted his original design; instead of the flat southern end being a stage area, it was turned into the main entrance with the curved end nearest Broad Street becoming the centre of attention, the magnificently carved Chancellor's Chair standing grandly at its mid-point, flanked on either side by carvings of the Proctors, the University's policemen. Sadly, the alignment of the building meant that the grand entrance was tucked between the building and the Divinity Schools, thus losing much of its impressive impact.

In fact, the Theatre has been used for many public performance over the years, mainly for musical recitals. It was here that George Frederick Handel and his consort played, prompting the Oxford historian, Thomas Hearne, to dismiss them as 'a lowsy crew of foreign fiddlers'.

Encaenia Procession
BROAD STREET

Every year in the Trinity (or Summer) term, one of the great Oxford traditions, the Encaenia, or 'Act', takes place, when honorary degrees are conferred on the deserving – be it in politics, the arts or sciences – in celebration of the end of the academic year. This ceremony begins with a procession of all the University authorities from the Chancellor down, walking in great state to the Sheldonian Theatre where the ceremony takes place. It is a magnificent sight, and one that has changed little over the centuries.

The bestowing of honorary degrees has always been a source of controversy; in 1809 the playwright and politician Sheridan was rejected by the votes of two hostile dons. He attended the ceremony anyway, and the clamour among the undergraduates on his appearance, was such that the ceremony could not continue until he had taken his place among those to be honoured; he later described it as one of the greatest moments of his life. Not so Margaret Thatcher, who was proposed for such an honour, only to be rejected by a majority of the professors in protest at her educational policies.

The Porter's Lodge
CORPUS CHRISTI COLLEGE

Like most of the Oxford colleges, Corpus Christi – pictured here – is approached through a Porter's Lodge, the main gatehouse to the College, and an essential part of every student's life. It is here that post is collected, that keys are kept and that information can be sought on every aspect of college life. Indeed, in many colleges the porters appear to

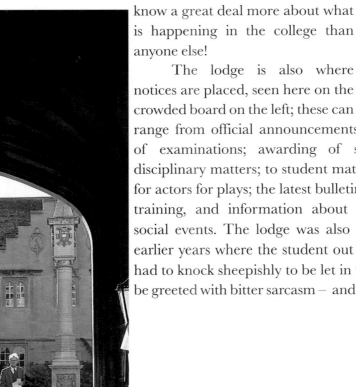

know a great deal more about what is happening in the college than anyone else!

The lodge is also where notices are placed, seen here on the crowded board on the left; these can range from official announcements: the results of examinations; awarding of scholarships; disciplinary matters; to student matters: appeals for actors for plays; the latest bulletins on rowing training, and information about forthcoming social events. The lodge was also the place in earlier years where the student out after curfew had to knock sheepishly to be let in to college, to be greeted with bitter sarcasm – and a heavy fine.

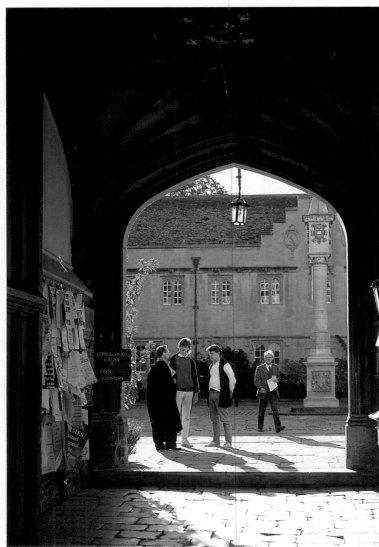

Degree Ceremony
SHELDONIAN THEATRE

The magnificent Sheldonian Theatre is the scene for a Degree Ceremony, when successful undergraduates become graduates, and where graduates receive their Doctorates or Fellowships. The different coloured gowns denote the area of study of the wearer; be it a Bachelor of Arts or of Science, they all define precisely the degree awarded.

Students at Oxford have two such ceremonies during their time at the University; this is the second, the first being Matriculation – the formal moment when they are accepted into the University and agree to be bound by its rules, and have their name entered into the books of their college.

One further eccentricity of the University, shared with Cambridge, is that the awarding of a Master's degree merely requires the graduate to wait seven years and then pay a nominal fee; as no examination is required, the Oxford Master merely has to place the letters (Oxon) after his or her title, to let the world know how it was achieved.

Examination Schools
HIGH STREET

Students stand nervously outside the Examination Schools on the High Street, waiting for the ominous moment when they are allowed in to the building to start the exams that will determine what they have to show for several years' study.

The Schools were built between 1876 and 1882, and were a result of the new zeal for reform in Victorian Oxford. Previously, exams had been entirely oral, a form dating back to the Middle Ages, but one which had become increasingly discredited and open to abuse. The introduction of written exams meant that the University could standardise the degrees given to students, although an oral test or 'viva' is still given to decide borderline cases; the possibility of college tutors favouring their own students could thus be outlawed. The undergraduates here are wearing 'sub-fusc', a suit and tie, with the appropriate academic gown which is compulsory for all examinations; the shorter gowns are worn by Commoners, the longer by Scholars – students who have won scholarships to the University.

Post-exam Celebrations
HIGH STREET

Students are likely to take two sets of exams during their time at Oxford: Moderations, or 'Mods', at the end of the first year, which only count towards a final degree in some courses; and Finals, which are the most important; the class of degree with which one leaves Oxford is decided here. The pressure on undergraduates has increased dramatically over the past few decades, with the competition of excellent universities throughout Britain and the dwindling jobs market making it essential to come away with a good degree; the days of a 'Gentleman's Third' are long past.

For many years this pressure was released on the last day of exams with a celebration with friends outside the Exam Schools; however, in recent times this became so rowdy that the High Street could be blocked for hours with carousing students, and the University authorities have now banned such lavish celebrations.

THE COLLEGES

From the very first educational halls established here in the Middle Ages have grown some of the finest buildings in England. Colleges, cloisters, quads and towers all represent their own unique history and traditions.

Queen's College
HIGH STREET

One of the grandest of all the Oxford colleges, with a Baroque splendour unmatched almost anywhere in Britain, Queen's College actually dates from the Middle Ages; it was founded in 1341, although building did not begin until 1352. The rudimentary quadrangle was finished by the end of the century, only to be swept away 300 years later by the architects George Clarke and, later, Nicholas Hawksmoor. Taking nearly 40 years to complete and helped by a substantial donation of money from Queen Caroline, George II's consort, the college is one of the high points of Oxford's classical architecture, and it is fitting that the cupola over the college entrance should contain a statue of Queen Caroline.

The list of famous students is a long one: rumour has it that Henry V studied at the medieval college, but certainly such luminaries as Edmund Halley the scientist, Jeremy Bentham the philosopher (who came to the college at the age of 12), Walter Pater and Joseph Addison the writers and in recent times, Rowan Atkinson of *Blackadder* fame all studied here.

New College Cloisters
QUEENS LANE

In one of Oxford University's great ironies, New College is actually one of its oldest colleges – founded in 1379 by William of Wykeham, Bishop of Winchester and later a Chancellor of England. The sweep of the Black Death through the city had caused a huge drop in the population, an instance that allowed Wykeham to buy the land in the east of Oxford and establish this particularly grand college. Its lavish scale also bears testimony to his role as surveyor of the new Windsor Castle, built for Edward III; certainly he was no stranger to grandiose schemes.

New College was larger than all the other fourteenth-century colleges combined, with about 70 Fellows, and its quadrangle was four times the size of Merton's Mob Quad, which had just been completed. The cloisters pictured here were unusual for a college, but were used for burial of

Fellows, one in ten of whom died within four years of Matriculation in the fifteenth century. The gardens contain the old city walls, the cloisters and the mound; all these are evidence of the grandeur of Wykeham's ambition.

Christ Church College
ST ALDATES

Originally called Cardinal College, Christ Church stands as an eloquent testament to the vaulting ambition of its initial founder, Cardinal Wolsey, and its subsequent benefactor, Henry VIII. Standing at the very south of the city, overlooking the Meadows which lead down to the river, and which bear its name, it is the grandest of all the colleges, with a reputation for educating those of rank, rather than of academic brilliance. Nevertheless, it numbers among its alumni Edward VII, Robert Peel, William Gladstone, John Ruskin, Lewis Carroll, John and Charles Wesley, and W. H. Auden.

Known as 'The House', the building was begun under the instruction of Wolsey, and was designed by the architects who had created his country house, Hampton Court. The main quadrangle, with its beautiful fountain statue of Mercury, was begun in 1525, and is now known as Tom Quad, because of the later gatehouse that stands on its west side; to the south is the Great Hall, resting on a vaulted undercroft, the largest and most impressive in either Oxford or Cambridge.

Pembroke College
ST ALDATES

One of the later colleges to be founded in Oxford's formative period, Pembroke was established in 1624 on the site of Broadgates Hall, a medieval academic institution, opposite the imposing grandeur of Christ Church. It is one of the smaller colleges, and was originally one of the poorest. It squatted for many years in the existing buildings, and the front quadrangle was not completed until 1679. Over the subsequent centuries, Pembroke has been remodelled and expanded, but in many ways it remains overshadowed by the giant over the road.

Pembroke can, however, boast one giant of its own: Samuel Johnson, the towering figure of eighteenth-century letters, was a student here, and became one of Oxford's most colourful characters. On being fined for not attending a lecture, he is said to have remarked to the lecturer: 'Sir, you have fined me twopence for a lecture that was not worth a penny'. His desk, teapot, books and a portrait by Reynolds are still in the College's possession.

St Edmund Hall

HIGH STREET

'Teddy Hall', as it is commonly known, is one of the smallest of the Oxford colleges and is tucked discreetly behind Queen's College. Although St Edmund Hall was not incorporated in to the University as a college until the middle part of this century, it was one of the few academic halls to survive the Middle Ages, and it actually dates back to the thirteenth century when it was named after a famous scholar of the time, Edmund of Abingdon. Halls like this were the earliest models for the modern colleges, but they developed in a different way, thanks to their smaller size and number of students.

By the seventeenth century, St Edmund was the only such hall still in existence; according to Thomas Salmon students lived like 'Gentlemen in a private family. There was not so much of that Submission and Ceremony observ'd, as in the houses that are incorporated.' Most of the architecture of the college dates back to the sixteenth and seventeenth centuries; in the centre of the quadrangle can be seen the well that was the Hall's only source of water until the late eighteenth century.

St Peter's College
NEW INN HALL STREET

Oxford's architecture incorporates a variety of styles, ranging from the Medieval to the Classical; St Peter's College manages to combine not only several styles, but also several different types of building, constructed for a variety of uses.

The College was established in 1929 as a 'private hall' by the Evangelical Bishop of Liverpool, F. J. Chavasse, a low-churchman keen to educate others in his own brand of Christianity. The site he chose on New Inn Hall Street had been in use for centuries, and he utilised the buildings that were already in position, including the church of St Peter-le-Bailey, seen here on the left, which became the College chapel. Its name refers back to its position as one of the northern gates of the medieval town, although the current building dates back only to 1874.

The new college took the name of its church, and also incoroporated Hannington Hall – an earlier educational establishment – and Wyaston House, the eighteenth-century offices of the Canal Company which became the Porter's Lodge; one of the great charms of the College is to be found in this eclectic mix of building styles.

University College
HIGH STREET

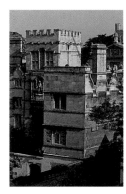

The grandly named and classically beautiful University College began its academic life as the poor relation of the other medieval colleges; even by comparison with Balliol it was impoverished and the magnificence of Merton was of an unimaginable scale. Univ, as it is now known, began with only four members (Merton had between 30 and 40) and no buildings of its own until the fourteenth century.

Unusually, the buildings they did attain in 1332 and over the succeeding years, were entirely demolished in the seventeenth century, after which time most of the current buildings were erected; even this building work was delayed for two decades by a lack of funding. As can be seen from the familiar presence of St Mary's Church and the Radcliffe Camera, the College is right in the heart of the University, on the High Street; it has been home to many famous people, from Robert Dudley, Earl of Leicester, Queen Elizabeth I's favourite to Clement

Atlee and Stephen Spender in this century. Its most famous son, however, remains the poet Shelley, who was sent down for atheism, but whose memorial is enshrined within the College.

Lady Margaret Hall
NORHAM GARDENS

The incorporation of women in to the University was a slow and hard-fought process; the battle has now been won, and virtually every college had become a co-educational institution by the 1980s. The gauntlet had been thrown down in earnest, however, a century earlier by the introduction of the women's halls. The first to open was 'a small hall or hostel in connection with the Church of England'; founded in a house leased from St John's, it became Lady Margaret Hall. In the same year, 1879, Somerville College was established for 11 students in Walton House, near the Radcliffe Infirmary.

Women were allowed to sit for most examinations, although they were awarded a diploma, not a degree, when they passed. The hostility towards them was in many places intense; as early as 1851 Samuel Sidney wrote 'the Oxford female is only of two kinds – prim and brazen. The latter we will not describe; the former seem to live in perpetual fear of being winked at, and are indescribable'. It was not until the late twentieth century that such attitudes were largely eradicated.

Somerville College
WOODSTOCK ROAD

Founded in 1879 for 11 female students, Somerville rapidly came to represent all that Oxford feared in the bluestocking; academic excellence and, in many cases, superiority. In 1920 women were finally permitted to receive degrees, and the men suddenly found real competition; an anonymous early twentieth-century rhyme reveals:

I spent all my time with a crammer,
And then only managed a gamma,
But the girl over there,
With the flaming red hair
Got an alpha plus easily – damn her!

Many men had been fearful that the granting of degree status to women was the first step in being forced to allow them the vote; so it is a nice irony that two of the twentieth century's leading stateswomen should both have been educated at Somerville: Indira Gandhi and Margaret Thatcher. Neither, one feels, would have put up with the patronising tone adopted by John Ruskin at the end of the nineteenth century: 'So glad to be old enough to be let come and have tea at Somerville, and to watch the girlies play at ball.'

Entrance to Brasenose College
RADCLIFFE SQUARE

Seen from the steps of the Bodleian Library, Brasenose College presents a stern face to the world outside; the gates in the middle of the wall are the only access to the college and are protected by the Porter's Lodge, that strictest of checkpoints.

One of the features of Oxford is the way the colleges have all been designed to be inward looking; right from the first foundations of Merton, Balliol and University Colleges in the thirteenth century, the buildings have all presented their harshest face to the world; it is only when one enters the colleges that their magic is revealed. This is partly due to the early designs of colleges, which used monastic establishments as their models, having no other institutions on which to draw, but it has remained a feature of college design right up until the present day.

One of the reasons that the famous 'dreaming spires' skyline is so well known is that it is almost the only wide-scale view of the University; the mysteries of each college lies within their walls, not openly on show to the rest of the world.

Brasenose College
RADCLIFFE SQUARE

uilt between 1509 and 1518, Brasenose stands at the academic heart of the city; the front quad pictured here is overshadowed by the bulk of the Radcliffe Camera immediately outside. Taking its name from the bronze lion's head that adorned its door, it was one of the fastest-growing of the colleges, and it was greatly extended in the seventeenth century when a new library and chapel were built to the south of this original quadrangle. The work took place between 1656 and 1663, and was almost the only construction carried out by any of the colleges during the Interregnum, the period between the death of Charles I and the Restoration. Further expansion took place in the late nineteenth century, when the college expanded still further, its southernmost buildings next to the High Street.

As well as boasting such illustrious occupants as Walter Pater, John Buchan, Earl Haig and William Golding, legend has it that Brasenose also taught Alexander Nowell, reputed to have invented bottled ale in the sixteenth century.

Corpus Christi College
MERTON STREET

Standing much as it did at its completion in about 1517, the front quadrangle of Corpus Christi, with its crenellated gate tower and elegant sundial surmounted by a pelican, is one of the least altered of all the colleges. Although the eighteenth-century president, Edward Turner, remodelled some of the college, and had constructed the elegant Fellows building to the south, overlooking Christ Church Meadow, it remains much as it was when it was founded by the blind bishop of Winchester, Richard Fox, a renaissance scholar much interested by the Classics.

Fox's plan for a tri-lingual library in Latin, Greek and English enormously impressed the Dutch scholar, Erasmus, who wrote in 1519: 'My mind foretells that in the future this college, like some holy temple dedicated to good learning, will be accounted among the chief glories of Britain . . . and that the spectacle of that tri-lingual library will in the future draw more persons to Oxford than Rome drew to herself of old.'

Tom Tower
CHRIST CHURCH COLLEGE

One of the most important and familiar of Oxford's landmarks, Tom Tower stands over the gateway to Christ Church College, which had been left unfinished on Cardinal Wolsey's fall from grace in 1529. It was built in 1681, designed by Christopher Wren – his last Oxford building – as a personal favour to the Dean of Christ Church, John Fell. The tower was built on Tudor lines 'to agree with the founder's work', and the new blends in so seamlessly with the old that it is hard to believe that the two are not of one design.

The tower houses the bell, Great Tom, that had previously hung in Osney Abbey, dissolved by Wolsey during the Reformation. Tom strikes 101 times every night at precisely five past nine, one chime for each of the original students of the college. It is this bell that Jude Fawley hears on his first night in Christminster in Hardy's *Jude the Obscure*: 'He must have made a mistake, he thought: it was meant for a hundred'; and it was this bell that used to announce to undergraduates that it was time for curfew.

St John's Canterbury Quadrangle
ST GILES

One of the great Classical triumphs of Oxford architecture, Canterbury Quad was built between 1631 and 1636 on the initiative of William Laud, Archbishop of Canterbury – a former President of the college and Chancellor of the University. It takes its inspiration from Renaissance Italy, with the two loggias on the west and east sides owing much to Florentine architecture. The eastern side pictured here was also designed to hold the library on its first floor, now called the Laud Library. The whole quadrangle is bedecked with statues and busts: of the Seven Virtues; the Seven Liberal Arts; the coats-of-arms of Charles I and the Archbishop; and bronze statues of the king and his queen,

Henrietta Maria, seen here.

The marriage of church and state is celebrated throughout the quadrangle; Laud further strengthened this connection with a banquet in 1636 for the King and Queen in the New Library, described by Anthony Wood as a dinner 'at which all the gallantry and beauties of the kingdom seemed to meet'. Such harmony was not to last, and both Laud and Charles were to lose their lives in the Civil War a decade later.

President's Garden Gate, St John's College
ST GILES

The opulence of St John's – in the design of its buildings, in its statuary; in its gardens – are proof enough of the college's enormous wealth, gained through donations and land ownership. At one point it was possible to walk from Oxford to Cambridge without ever leaving St John's land; it was the bequests of this land that made the colleges so rich and enabled such elaborate building schemes to take place.

If the colleges were rich, the students were frequently immensely poor. From Chaucer's clerk, as thin and threadbare as his horse, with 'litel gold in cofre', to William Pitt the Elder in 1727, writing to appease his father for 'the extravagance of my expenses', the story of Oxford's undergraduate has been one of hand-to-mouth existence; on his fall from grace in 1534 Thomas More reassured his children that they would not starve: 'May we yet like poor scholars of Oxford go a begging with our bags and wallets and sing Salve Regina at rich mens dores.' Modern students do not face quite the same grinding poverty, although eavesdropping on any conversation at the King's Arms will quickly unearth a string of complaints about the inadequacy of the grant.

Saint Catherine's College
MANOR ROAD

Saint Catherine's College, seen here from the west over the water gardens, was built between 1960 and 1964, and represents the high point of the international style of Modernism in Oxford. Created when it became clear that the St Catherine's Society for Non-Collegiate Students had outgrown its premises in St Aldate's, the then-Master Alan Bullock employed the Danish architect Arne Jacobsen to create a wholly new college, albeit one adhering to a quadrangular layout and with traditional staircase entry to the rooms.

Using a substantial amount of plate-glass and concrete, the harsh effect of the buildings is softened by the water gardens rich in plant life, and the low brick walls in the gardens, which give a feeling of space unusual in an Oxford college. Even so, the critic Reyner Banham described the finished buildings in 1964's *Architectural Review as* 'the best motel in Oxford'. However much it divides critics, St Catz remains one of England's most notable examples of modern architecture.

Wadham College
PARKS ROAD

Named after its founders, Sir Nicholas and Dorothy, Lady Wadham, whose statues can be seen in the quadrangle, the college was founded in 1610 to the north of the city wall, on the site of an old Augustinian Friary. Sir Nicholas died in 1609, and it was left to his widow, a formidable 75-year-old, to see through the formation of the college.

Although she was accused in 1615 of being a Catholic, and came from an old Catholic family, Dorothy insisted on the College being run on very strict Anglican lines. Wadham was built to a similar design as the medieval colleges, including an open-roofed hall, seen here. The Chapel is firmly in the tradition of the High Church, although the chancel windows are filled with painted glass from Germany, unusual in a Protestant church. The Somerset workmen brought in by Lady Wadham, led by master mason William, made a fine job; even today the College is in an excellent state of repair.

Keble College
PARKS ROAD

Seen here bathed in autumn sunshine, Keble is one of the most distinctive of all the Oxford colleges, and the one that has most divided critical opinion. Situated to the north of the city centre, on the edge of the Parks, it was the first new college in Oxford since the founding of Wadham. Built between 1868 and 1882 to a design by William Butterfield and named after John Keble, the Anglican founder of the Oxford Movement, it is a masterpiece of Victorian Gothic, using bricks of a multitude of colours, rather than the traditional stone, and incorporating a chapel that draws on the traditions of Italian churches like Siena, rather than the customary French influence. Ablaze with gold, stained glass and mosaic, it is unlike anything else in Oxford.

The poet, Gerard Manley Hopkins, wrote to Butterfield in 1877, 'I do not think this generation will ever much admire it', and the truth of this statement was borne out by subsequent criticism, one critic likening the college to a dinosaur in a fairisle sweater. Butterfield himself, however, remained unrepentant: 'I set small store by popularity, and intend … to take the responsibility of thinking for myself.'

Mansfield College
MANSFIELD ROAD

Created as a direct result of the loosening of religious rules in the late-nineteenth century, Mansfield was one of the first of the non-Anglican religious colleges which sprang up in Oxford after the lifting of the Anglican monopoly in 1871. Beginning in Birmingham as a training college for ministers, the college moved to Oxford in 1886, to this pretty site with attractive gardens between Holywell Street and the Parks. It was designed by Basil Champneys, one of the leading exponents of late-Victorian Gothic architecture in Oxford.

As the first students lived out of the college, Champneys was able to use space freely. Using Tudor-Gothic designs, he set the College around a large, open-ended quadrangle, with a chapel, hall and a purely decorative gate-house, as well as a large library modelled partly on a Medieval tithe barn, extravagantly painted.

Mansfield remains an excellent example of how Oxford's traditional college building was carried on through the centuries; standing in its garden in the sun, it could date from almost any era of the University's history.

Wolfson College
NORTH OXFORD

During the 1960s the student population of the University soared, and new colleges had to be established to cope with the increasing numbers. Like St Catherine's in the early part of the decade, Wolfson College was built to meet this demand, on a site on the banks of the Cherwell in the heart of North Oxford. Named after its main benefactor, the Wolfson Foundation, the college was built between 1969 and 1974 by the architects Philip Powell and J. H. Moya, who were responsible for many of Oxford's new buildings in the 1960s.

One of the first colleges to make substantial provision for married students – a daring innovation at the time – Wolfson's buildings were designed, according to one Fellow, 'to be on a scale suited to their surroundings and suited also to their human occupants'. Although it has many aspects in common with St Catherine's, Wolfson has gone further in softening the hard lines of the new architecture, using water, trees and lawns, seen here bathed in spring sunshine.

Hertford College
NEW COLLEGE LANE

Situated right in the heart of academic Oxford, in the shadow of the Radcliffe Camera and St Mary's Church, Hertford has had a chequered history. Originally a seventeenth-century institution called Hart Hall, the college of the leading Metaphysical poet and Dean of St Pauls, John Donne, it was established as a college in 1740. However, financial hardship forced the college to sell its buildings and assets to Magdalen Hall in 1820, whose own buildings had been badly damaged by fire.

Refounded in 1874, following a substantial financial gift from the banker Charles Baring, the college went through a very thorough process of remodelling, using the inspiration of Renaissance Italy, the chateaux of the Loire in France and the existing buildings of previous incarnations. The college of Thomas Hobbes, the seventeenth-century philosopher; Charles James Fox, the politician; and the essential Oxford novelist, Evelyn Waugh, author of *Brideshead Revisited,* Hertford retains, for all its history, a strong sense of the uniqueness of Oxford.

Maison Français
NORHAM ROAD

The Maison Français nestles amid the Victorian villas and leafy roads of North Oxford, built in the early 1960s in the Modernist style by the French architect Jacques Laurent. It is almost featureless in its simplicity and its geometric shapes, but it nonetheless uses, as so many of the colleges do, the beauty of the trees and lawns to disguise its anonymity.

The school for French Studies is a testament to the rapid growth in both the number of students and areas of study in the latter half of this century. Oxford has moved with the times in embracing all areas of study, appreciating that the place of a modern university is to prepare for the real world and to accept the existence of a global village; all a very far cry from its medieval past when the study of the Classics was the only discipline open to a scholar, and all studies were conducted in Latin.

Worcester College
WORCESTER STREET

Located on the west side of the city, Worcester stands on the site of the fifteenth-century Gloucester College, a Benedictine monastic order, which largely disappeared when the current college was founded in 1714. However, some of the monks' rooms remain as one side of the beautiful, asymmetrical quadrangle, facing the long eighteenth-century residential building which we see here. Much of the architecture of Worcester was suggested by the celebrated architect Nicholas Hawksmoor, but a shortage of funding meant that the College took so long to build that a whole string of designers were eventually employed and the whole project was never completed.

The library of Worcester was designed by George Clarke, and contains many treasures, not least theatre designs by Inigo Jones which have been used as the basis for the Globe Theatre. Worcester's two most celebrated alumni demonstrate the widespread reach of Oxford, boasting as it does Thomas de Quincey, the author of *Confessions of an Opium Eater*, and Rupert Murdoch, the twentieth-century media baron.

Ruskin School of Drawing and Fine Art
HIGH STREET

One of the most celebrated art schools in the world, the Ruskin was originally built for an entirely different purpose. Constructed on part of the site of an old inn, the Angel, the building was first used as a base for students at the University who could not afford college fees, a use which Ruskin himself no doubt applauded. Designed by Thomas Graham Jackson, one of the most important late-Victorian architects in Oxford, it now stands as a permanent memorial to one of Oxford's most famous sons.

John Ruskin was born in 1819 and entered Christ Church in 1837, where he quickly gained fame as a critic of art and architecture, and as a poet. He became Professor of Art in 1869, and an honorary fellow of Corpus Christi in 1884, and his lectures and writings attracted an enormous following. Although he later fell out with the University authorities, his legacy in Oxford can be felt everywhere, not least in his passionate sense of social justice: 'that beauty which is indeed a joy forever, must be a joy for all'.

Merton College Mob Quad
MERTON STREET

Walter de Merton set out his new college along the lines of a monastery as there was little idea at this time of what a college should look like. The buildings were put up one at a time with no real overall design; Mob Quad, seen here from above, evolved in to its present form as more buildings were added to the college. The north and east buildings were constructed as chambers for the members in the first years of the fourteenth century; the south and west ranges were not added until 1373–78, together with more chambers and a library on the upper floor. Each chamber was designed for four occupants, with communal sleeping areas and a partitioned section for each student's study; although it is crowded by  today's standards, it represented luxury compared to other Medieval institutions.

Just as the actual buildings had no real blueprint, nor did the collegiate system, and it is in the original statutes of Merton that we can see the beginnings of what was to become college life at Oxford.

Magdalen College
HIGH STREET

One of the most beautiful of the Oxford colleges, Magdalen (pronounced Maudlin) College stands at the eastern end of the city, and it is over Magdalen Bridge, with its Classical structure dwarfed by Magdalen Tower, that the visitor from London first arrives in the town.

Magdalen was founded in 1458 by William Waynflete, a cleric destined to become Bishop of Winchester and Chancellor of England, and a man of enormous wealth; Magdalen was one of the richest foundations of all the colleges. It contains a wonderful mixture of architectural styles, from the Medieval to the eighteenth-century grandeur of the New Building; from the fifteenth-century cloisters and bell tower, seen here, to the Victorian Gothic of St Swithin's Quadrangle.

The college numbers among its alumni the philosopher Thomas Hobbes; the future King Edward VIII; the composer Ivor Novello; the Poet Laureate John Betjeman; and Oscar Wilde. Its most famously dissatisfied son remains the historian, Edward Gibbon, who wrote: 'I spent fourteen months at Magdalen College; they proved the fourteen months the most idle and unprofitable of my whole life.'

St Antony's College
WOODSTOCK ROAD

Set in the leafy roads of north Oxford, St Antony's college is an extraordinary combination of the old and the new. The college was founded as late as 1950 but stands on the site of an earlier convent, the Convent of Holy Trinity. Thanks to the Oxford Movement led by Cardinal Newman, it became possible to create Anglican religious communities, and Holy Trinity was established in 1864 by Marian Hughes, the first woman to take religious vows in England since the Reformation. It was built between 1866 and 1868 in the Victorian Gothic style, although the beautiful chapel, the spire of which is visible in the background, was modelled more on French designs.

This chapel is now the library of St Antony's, a college founded by the Frenchman Antonin Besse as a centre for international studies in the fevered atmosphere of Cold War Europe, using the original convent buildings. Between 1968 and 1970 the Hall and Common Room block were created, an example of modern Expressionism at its most extreme, with its cube structure; the contrast with the nineteenth-century convent could not be more pronounced, and is a good example of Oxford architecture's ability to incorporate many diverse cultures.

Exeter College Chapel
TURL STREET

The graceful spire of Exeter College chapel is one of the many glories of the Oxford skyline; construction of the new chapel began in 1856 to a design by George Gilbert Scott, architect of the Martyrs' Memorial. Frequently compared to the Sainte-Chapelle in Paris, due to its height and soaring lines, the new chapel replaced the existing seventeenth-century chapel at substantial cost; each of Exeter's Fellows donated a full year's salary towards the cost of the building.

By the mid-nineteenth century Exeter had become one of the most popular colleges in the University, and it can lay claim to many famous scholars and tutors: J. R. R. Tolkien, author of *Lord of the Rings* was a Fellow here; the great screen actor Richard Burton came here in the 1940s; and more recently, the author Martin Amis. Perhaps most significantly, it was home to two of the great Pre-Raphaelites: William Morris and Sir Edward Burne-Jones, and the college is still blessed with many designs and paintings by both these famous artists.

Nuffield College
WEST OXFORD

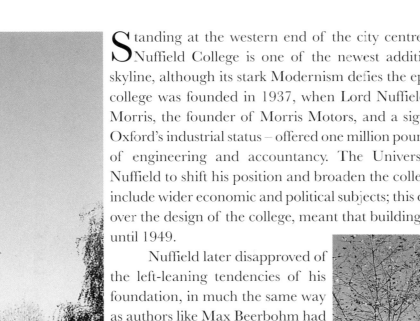

Standing at the western end of the city centre, the modern spire of Nuffield College is one of the newest additions to the celebrated skyline, although its stark Modernism defies the epithet 'dreaming'. The college was founded in 1937, when Lord Nuffield – originally William Morris, the founder of Morris Motors, and a significant contributer to Oxford's industrial status – offered one million pounds to establish a school of engineering and accountancy. The University authorities forced Nuffield to shift his position and broaden the college's academic focus to include wider economic and political subjects; this dispute, and arguments over the design of the college, meant that building did not actually begin until 1949.

Nuffield later disapproved of the left-leaning tendencies of his foundation, in much the same way as authors like Max Beerbohm had disapproved of the effect of industry on the city; it is ironic that Nuffield's college did much to improve the environs of west Oxford, while his factories had an exactly opposite effect in the east.

Lincoln College
TURL STREET

The ivy-covered quadrangle of Lincoln College is an almost perfect example of most people's image of an Oxford college; a quiet grove of academe in the middle of a bustling city, with scholars poring over books in their studies, overlooking a small but immaculate lawn, and closed off from the world outside by high walls and a strong gatehouse.

The college itself was founded in 1427 by Richard Fleming, Bishop of Lincoln, from whom it takes its name, and has always been one of the smaller colleges in the University, prevented from expanding partly by its position in the very centre of the city. At its foundation it housed only the Rector and seven graduate Fellows, and because of this, it has never attained the magnificence of a Christ Church or a Balliol. It does, however, boast one of the finest libraries in the University, in the former All Saints Church, whose magnificent spire is one of the most prominent of the dreaming spires of Oxford legend.

Oriel College
ORIEL SQUARE

One of the earliest of Oxford's colleges, Oriel lies just to the north-east of Merton, in the square which now bears its name. It was founded in 1326, one of the smaller establishments in the University, with fewer than a dozen members at first; even today it remains one of Oxford's smaller colleges.

The cramped Medieval buildings were mostly replaced in the first half of the seventeenth century to accomodate the increasing number of undergraduates and Fellows; and the unknown designer also included two statues of kings, surmounted by a representation of the Virgin and Child; these were hidden during the Commonwealth, as their High Anglicanism was thought to be dangerous.

Oriel has been home to many famous names, as diverse as Walter Raleigh, Beau Brummel and Cecil Rhodes, and the writer, C. S. Lewis took his exams here. He wrote home of the good and bad aspects of the college: 'The place has surpassed my wildest dreams; I never saw anything so beautiful, especially on these frosty nights; though in the Hall of Oriel where we take our papers it is fearfully cold. We have most of us tried, with varying degrees of success, to write in our gloves.'

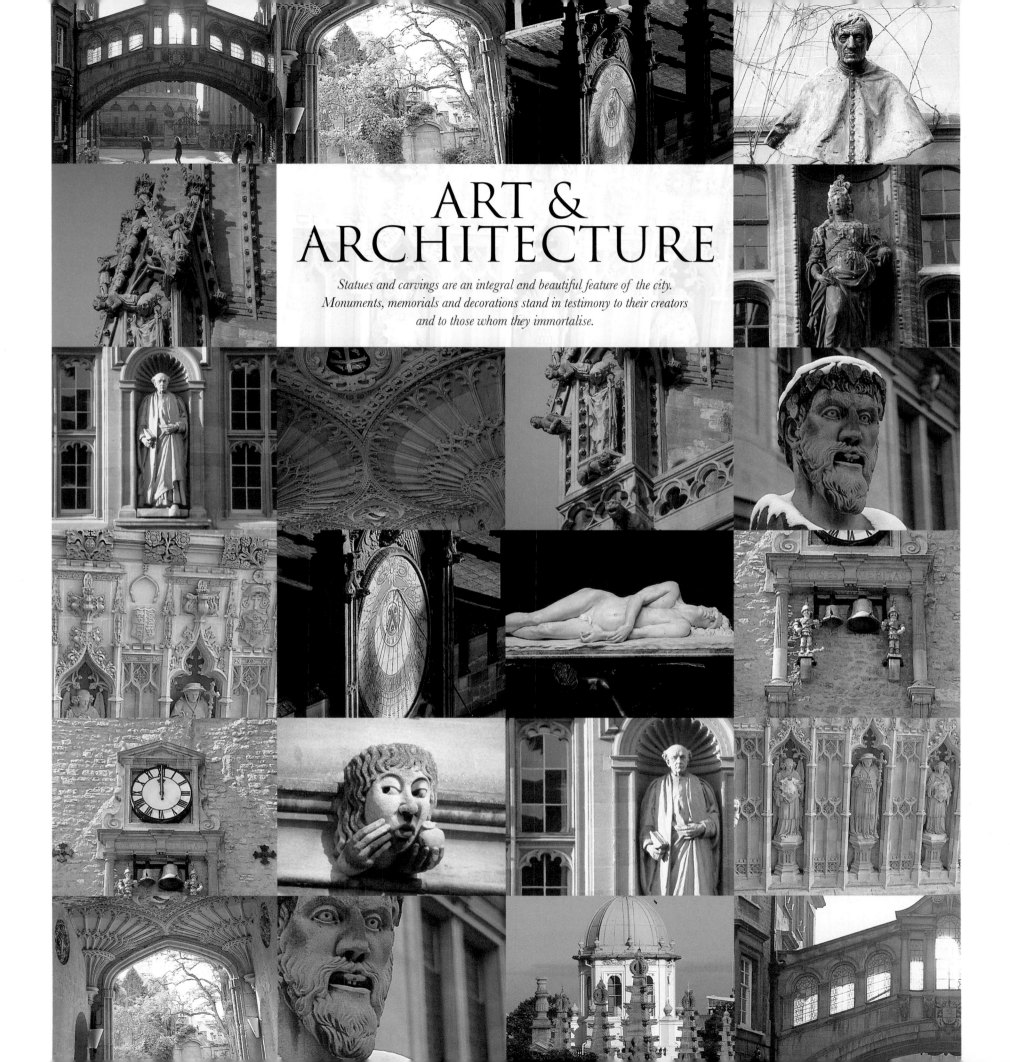

ART &
ARCHITECTURE

Statues and carvings are an integral and beautiful feature of the city.
Monuments, memorials and decorations stand in testimony to their creators
and to those whom they immortalise.

Shelley Memorial
UNIVERSITY COLLEGE

Oxford's tradition of honouring its favourite sons is, in this memorial to the drowned poet, laced with irony, for Percy Bysshe Shelley was actually sent down (expelled) from University College in 1811, after he jointly published an anti-religious tract, *The Necessity of Atheism*. Known from his schooldays as 'mad Shelley', he went on to become one of the most important poets of the Romantic movement, leaving behind a prodigious canon of work after his tragically early death at the age of 30.

This touching statue was created by Onslow Ford for the Protestant Cemetery in Rome, who refused it on the grounds of 'vulgarity'; it is now housed in the front quadrangle of University College, in a memorial designed by Basil Champneys in 1892–93. Lit from above, the memorial is also approached from above, giving the figure the impression of being underwater. Its languid form is fitting to both the poet's lifestyle, and to the late nineteenth-century ethos that shaped it. Despite its critics, it remains a moving tribute to one of Oxford's most important figures.

Cardinal Newman Memorial
TRINITY COLLEGE

As with the Shelley Memorial, the statue to John Henry Newman is another example of Oxford honouring those who caused it most aggravation, for Cardinal Newman, one of the giants of Oxford's history, was actually forced to resign from the University in 1841, because of his High Church religious views.

Newman had gone up to Trinity College, where this bust is situated, in 1816 at the age of 15, gained his degree at the age of 20 and was made a Fellow of Oriel College. He was also made vicar of St Mary's, the University church, in 1828, and he used this position to advocate the controversial beliefs that became known as the Oxford Movement, with Newman and Keble at its head. Although a shy man, he was a brilliant speaker and his sermons drew vast audiences, and inevitably brought him in to confrontation with the religious authorities. After leaving Oxford he became a Roman Catholic and set up an oratory in Birmingham; 32 years later he was finally forgiven by his old University, and he was elected an honorary Fellow of Trinity College, where his career had begun.

Fan Vaulting
UNIVERSITY COLLEGE

The influence of Gothic architecture can be seen everywhere in University Oxford, nowhere more beautifully than in this fan vaulting under the gate tower in Radcliffe Quadrangle in University College. When the early eighteenth-century benefactor stipulated that the 'new work should be answerable to the [17th century] front already built', the builders readily agreed – even though Classical design was the height of fashion throughout the rest of Britain. This vaulting was added so carefully and precisely, that it seems to date from a previous century.

That the influence of the European Gothic cathedrals should be so strong throughout the University is not really be a surprise, for the intertwining of learning and religion that characterised Medieval Europe is the prevailing culture of Oxford. It goes right back to the very foundation of the University, which was set up to be a centre of learning for monks and the clergy, and it is no coincidence that Oxford University has been a centre for religious discussion and disputation for all of its long history.

Dean Liddell Monument
CHRIST CHURCH COLLEGE

Framed between two leaded windows in Christ Church College stands this memorial to Dean Henry Liddell, who, unlike Shelley and Newman, led a life of exemplary University and religious service. His very conformity has meant that his fame is largely forgotten, like so many University men over the centuries, who have nonetheless guided and helped the life of the city.

Born in 1829, he was educated at King's College School in London and took his degree from Christ Church in 1850. Ordained in to the clergy in 1853 at the age of 24, he went on to become Vice-Principal of St Edmund Hall, a member of the University Council three times, a Doctor of Divinity and in 1870, a Canon of St Paul's Cathedral in London. Here, his sermons became an essential part of London religious life, and most were published. He was created Chancellor of St Paul's in 1886, and was still preaching up until his death in 1890. Liddell's is a life which well epitomises nineteenth-century Oxford's ideal of service.

Statue of Cardinal Wolsey
CHRIST CHURCH COLLEGE

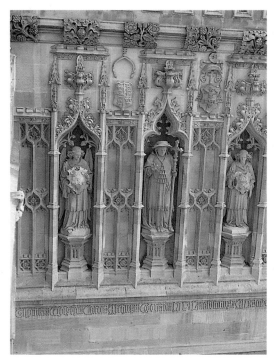

As with so many of the memorials and statues that grace the University buildings, there is a bitter irony in this memorial to Cardinal Wolsey on the tower of Christ Church College, for the College was originally planned by the Cardinal himself around 1525 and was originally to have been called Cardinal's College. The arrogant grandeur of Wolsey's designs can be seen in the way he financed the project by tightly suppressing several religious houses and by demolishing a church and much of a monastery to the south of the city in order to make room for his college.

Little of the building was completed in 1529 when Wolsey fell from Henry VIII's favour, and the King took on the founding of the new college himself, christening it Christ Church and removing all evidence of Wolsey's involvement. This was a large task as, according to the French Ambassador of the time, 'there is hardly a stone from the top of the buildings to the very foundations where his blazoned armorial is not sculpted'.

Carfax Clock
ST MARTIN'S CHURCH TOWER

Midday at the mid-point of University life. In the same way that cartographers consider Marble Arch in London the actual centre of the city, so the Carfax crossroads is considered the epicentre of the University, even though it stands slightly to the west of the town. It is from this spot that the distance is measured which determines how far out of the city undergraduates may reside, and from the clock on St Martin's Church tower is measured the accurate University time.

Time has become a less important matter in the last decades of University life, as undergraduates are no longer bound by a curfew, but within living memory the peal of bells from Tom Tower would send students racing for their colleges before the gates were locked. To be caught outside after curfew would entail a difficult climb over the college walls, and possibly even being caught by the dreaded proctors and reported to the College authorities.

Emperor's Head
SHELDONIAN THEATRE

The classical designs of the Sheldonian Theatre, brilliantly executed by Christopher Wren, were slightly spoiled by the University authorities' decision to turn the building around – making the back of the building face the outside world – and by the fact that the public funds he had expected never actually materialised. It is, therefore, the curved back of the building which faces Broad Street and the world, with its line of Emperors' heads on pillars glaring down on the passing tourists.

These are properly called 'herms', human heads on plinths, and are a Classical Roman style, derived from Roman boundary posts. They have, however, been known as 'the heads' for countless generations, and it is these heads that glower so unforgivingly on the Duke of Dorset in Max Beerbohm's *Zuleika Dobson* as he races to his doom. By the 1950s, when the Sheldonian was refaced, the heads had been so badly damaged by time and pollution that they were unrecognisable as human. They were actually replaced between 1970 and 1972, the originals having been declared irrecoverable.

All Soul's Sundial
ALL SOUL'S COLLEGE

Illuminated by the evening sun, Christopher Wren's baroque sundial has told the time to generations of All Soul's Fellows, and in its Latin inscription, *Pereunt et imputantur*, has exhorted them to greater efforts – 'the hours pass and must be accounted for'.

Another of Oxford's greatest sons, Wren is remembered chiefly as an architect, notably designing the Sheldonian Theatre and Tom Tower, and most famously, St Paul's Cathedral in London. He was also an astronomer and geometrician of distinction, and was fascinated by dials and meteorological devices, this being one of the most ornate. Wren came up to Oxford to study at Wadham, gained his degree in 1651, and was elected a Fellow of All Soul's after gaining his MA. He was Professor of Astronomy from 1661 to 1673, although after the Great Fire of London in 1666, he spent most of his time in the capital, helping with the rebuilding of the city. He did return, however, in 1681 to complete the main entrance to Christ Church, and it was then that the famous Tom Tower came into being.

Sheldonian Cupola
SHELDONIAN THEATRE

One of the most familiar of Oxford's landmarks the cupola, or dome, of the Sheldonian Theatre is thought by many to be the work of Christopher Wren, the building's architect. In fact it is a much later replacement, designed by Edward Blore, constructed in 1837–38, and thought by some to be out of proportion with the rest of the building.

Wren's original dome was much smaller, due to the building being used by the University Press, housed in the basement. It was considered essential to store books in the roof of the new building; this meant Wren had to provide an ungainly attic storey and a row of oval windows above the balustrade level, none of which were included in his original design. The very nature of this storage space meant that Wren's cupola at the apex of the roof was rather small, and when the Press moved from the Theatre to the Clarendon Building in 1713, it became possible to change the dimensions. That it took over a century to decide to do this is an enduring testament to the reverence in which Wren's work was held.

Bridge of Sighs
HERTFORD COLLEGE

The evening sun glints through the glass of Hertford College's covered bridge, with the rounded form of the Sheldonian Theatre in the background. As a direct result of Hertford's chequered history of foundation, closure, refoundation and the diversity of architectural styles that have been incorporated in to the college as a result, it comes as no surprise that the college is divided into two separate units, split by New College Lane.

When T. G. Jackson was redesigning the college at the beginning of this century, the decision was made to join the newer accommodation blocks on the north side of the lane to the older part of the college to the south, and it is typical of his flamboyant style that he should have chosen to model his bridge on an Italian Renaissance covered bridge; it was built between 1913 and 1914, and finished just before the outbreak of the First World War. Although it is, in fact, most similar in style to Venice's Rialto Bridge, it has been known to generations of Oxford students as 'the Bridge of Sighs'.

Queen Anne's Statue
UNIVERSITY COLLEGE

Standing over the High Street, defaced by pollution from the steady stream of cars, Queen Anne gazes out from the façade of University College. Although the Queen herself was no great friend to the University, she is celebrated here by one of the University's greatest benefactors – her personal physician, John Radcliffe. Their relationship foundered after he termed her distemper 'nothing but the vapours', and he refused to visit her on her deathbed, but her patronage of Radcliffe enabled him to be of enormous benefit to the University.

He was the donor who enabled University College to be extended in the early eighteenth century; his trustees founded the Radcliffe Observatory; the Radcliffe Infirmary, Oxford's first hospital; and his name is remembered today in the John Radcliffe Hospital, Oxford's modern hospital. Most famously, he was the founder of the Radcliffe Camera, one of Oxford's most enduring and famous landmarks, leaving a grant of £40,000 for the work after his death in 1714. This beautiful building, begun by Hawksmoor and finished by James Gibbs, stands as an enduring monument to one of Oxford's greatest citizens.

Gargoyle
CHURCH BUILDING

Originally designed to frighten devils away from religious institutions and to safeguard worshippers, gargoyles in Medieval churches were intended to be as hideous and as terrifying as possible. Over the centuries most have come to be considered rather more endearing than grotesque, and this fellow, whispering furtively about some University gossip, would barely frighten a child. Indeed, the famous gargoyles around the centre of the University are now internationally beloved, more in the style of Renaissance cherubs, and their mischievous faces adorn postcards, tea-towels, place-mats and a whole host of other tourist memorabilia.

Many are thought to be portraits of University characters, either dons or students, their mannerisms preserved forever in stone, and although a few are genuinely old, most date from more recent times, many appearing in the last century – some even in this one, created to amuse or provoke, rather than to scare away the legions of Satan.

Church Carvings
ST MARY'S CHURCH

High on the spire of St Mary's the sun turns the pendant statues and carvings gold, and throws into relief the faces of the gargoyles. The spire is one of the most famous landmarks in the Oxford skyline, and is of unusually lavish design. It dates back to the early-fourteenth century; the statues are of saints, each protected by an overhanging gable with extravagant pairs of pinnacles at each corner of the tower; the carving is of a very high degree of craftsmanship.

With the passing centuries the building has undergone many face-lifts as early as 1490 the Chancellor of the University was bemoaning the perilous state of the masonry, and in the early-sixteenth century, according to the English traveller John Leland, a great gale blew down some of the pinnacles, which had to be replaced. One cannot help but wonder at the dedication of the craftsmen who set these statues here, so precisely detailed, yet so far from the view of the naked eye on the ground.

GARDENS & PARKS

Hidden between the bright stone of the colleges and churches of Oxford lies a plethora of rich parks, gardens and landscaped lawns. They are havens of peace and tranquillity amidst the hurried life of the city.

Sunset
WORCESTER COLLEGE LAKE

Worcester College boasts one of the most beautiful gardens of all the University colleges, and this view of Worcester College Lake at sunset in mid-winter sums up the tranquillity and serenity of the Oxford college gardens. One of the eternal joys of the University is the ability to escape the bustle and noise of the city, to study, to play, or simply to reflect, in the middle of nature. It is an ideal the Classical civilisations aspired to: *rus in urbe* – an integral part of the magic of Oxford.

Worcester's gardens and lake are a rich part of Oxford's dramatic heritage, and every summer plays are staged here by the students. In one memorable production of *The Tempest*, duckboards were set just beneath water level, so that the spirit Ariel could run directly across the surface of the water into the sunset. The only drawback is Worcester's proximity to the railway station tannoy, leading one wit to pronounce of the college, 'c'est magnifique, mais ce n'est pas la gare'.

Gardens
ST HILDA'S COLLEGE

St Hilda's College was founded in 1893, at the height of the sweeping changes that brought women into the University as equals to the men. It was established in the south-east of the town, just beyond Magdalen Bridge on the eastern bank of the Cherwell, in an existing eighteenth-century building, previously known as Cowley House. Although one of the more recently founded Oxford colleges, it boasts one of the most attractive locations of all.

Access to the river is a major attraction for residents of the city; noise and bustle of life in the centre makes escape to the quiet and solitude of the rivers particularly appealing. John Keats, fresh from London, records in his diaries, 'we have had regularly a boat on the Isis, and explored all the streams about, which are more in number than your eyelashes . . . there is one particularly nice nest . . . in which we have read Wordsworth and talked as maybe'.

Magdalen Deer Park
MAGDALEN COLLEGE

One of the most surprising of the Oxford college gardens, Magdalen Deer Park, as its name suggests, affords the visitor wonderful views of red deer, roaming freely about the park, so used to human contact by now that they are tame enough to take food from the hand. The number of deer varies from year to year, but they are afforded great respect by the College and the students, and are frequently to be found in the College quadrangles, grazing on the immaculately manicured lawns, having strayed in from the Park.

The deer park is one of Oxford's wilder gardens, officially called Magdalen Grove, stretching down to Addison's Walk on the banks of the Cherwell; it was the inspiration for a poem written by John Keats, in 1819:

> There are plenty of trees,
> And plenty of ease,
> And plenty of fat deer for Parsons;
> And when it is venison,
> Short is the benison , -
> Then each on a leg or thigh fastens.

The Parks
NORTH OXFORD

Situated to the north of the city centre, the University Parks are the playing fields of the University, most specifically used for cricket. Seen here in spring, with buttercups scattered in the long grass, and dominated by the Gothic form of Keble Chapel, they are a large expanse of recreational park, open to everyone, unlike most of the college gardens which are closed to visitors, except at certain times.

It is in the Parks that the University cricket team play their home fixtures, and by tradition it is at the Parks that the first match of the county season takes place. The days when the University was a County side to be reckoned with have, however, sadly long passed, as the modern game has demanded more and more professionalism, and the opportunities for the gifted amateur have diminished. The elegant pavilion, designed in 1880 by Thomas Jackson, remains a lasting monument to a more gentlemanly age.

Gardens
TRINITY COLLEGE

The formality of Trinity's gardens – the immaculately mown lawn with its precise stripes, the carefully raked pathway and the wisteria pruned back to the walls – are all firmly in keeping with the Classical form of the late seventeenth-century chapel which overlooks it. The gardens are a fine example of the results of the friendly rivalry between Oxford college gardeners, who take enormous pride in their work and each struggle to maintain the most beautiful and impressive landscapes.

One of the main differences between Oxford and Cambridge, 'the other place', is the privacy of the Oxford gardens; most tend to be kept behind closed doors within the walls of the colleges, and there is nowhere in the city the equivalent to 'the Backs', Cambridge's landscaped gardens along the banks of the Cam. Although this means the centre of Oxford can seem more a collection of brickwork than scenic views, it also allows the sudden surprise of a secret garden, the intake of breath as one comes across such beauty in the middle of a city.

Gardens with Bluebells
WADHAM COLLEGE

Situated in the very centre of the city, the garden of Wadham is a wonderful shock to the visitor, ablaze with colour, with its bluebells and blossom shimmering in the spring sunshine, a magnificent copper beech casting a shadow over the lawns.

The diarist, Francis Kilvert, revisiting his old college in 1864, a decade after his graduation, describes the garden: 'I wandered round to Wadham gardens. All was usual, the copper beech still spread a purple gloom in the corner, the three glorious limes swept their luxuriant foliage flat upon the sward, the great poplars towered like a steeple, the laburnum showered its golden rain by the quiet cloisters and the wisteria still hung its blue flower clusters upon the garden wall. The fabric of the college was unchanged, the grey chapel walls still rose fair and peaceful from the green turf.' Should Kilvert have visited again today, he would have found little changed, and it is typical of Oxford that its joys and perfection should have remained unmarred over the last one hundred years.

Gardens
NEW COLLEGE

The garden at New College, one of the largest of any of the Medieval colleges, is seen here in the morning sunshine looking towards the college. It was one of the first gardens to be laid out, with a viewing-mound built in 1594 and elaborated on in 1648: 'perfected with stepps of stone and setts for the hedges about the walke'. Significantly, the diarist Celia Fiennes remarks that the garden was 'new-makeing' on her visit in 1694, and she is certainly referring to the construction, between 1682 and 1707, of the Garden Quadrangle, seen here from the east.

The first open-ended courtyard to be built in Oxford, this was designed to look out over the elaborate gardens, which contained, according to Fiennes, 'a large bason of water in the middle, and little walkes and mazes and round mounts for the schollars to divert themselves in'. Although these delights have mostly disappeared over the centuries, it still remains one of Oxford's most beautiful gardens.

Gardens
BALLIOL COLLEGE

Seen here looking north towards the Hall, designed by Alfred Waterhouse in 1873, Balliol has one of the smaller gardens in Oxford, unsurprisingly for a college at the very centre of the city, flanked by Broad Street and St Giles. The Hall is one of the largest in Oxford, and is complimented on the south and east sides by the same architect's rebuilding of the original fifteenth-century quadrangle. The height of the buildings, coupled with Waterhouse's use of Bath stone and dark mortar, makes the garden seem smaller than it actually is, and gives it a brooding quality very removed from the more open spaces of most other colleges.

It is also less formally laid out than many other Oxford gardens, with flower beds overflowing with shrubs and smaller trees dotting the lawn; the daffodils seen here are springing up around an object known as 'Devorguilla's Tomb', reputedly the resting-place of an Anglo-Saxon princess.

University Arboretum
NUNEHAM COURTENAY

About six miles south of the city lies the University arboretum, in the gardens of Nuneham Courtenay, a beautiful estate overlooking the Thames, with a prospect of the dreaming spires to the north. It is here that many of Oxford's botanical studies take place and many of its rarer specimens are kept, since the Botanical Gardens in the city itself do not have adequate space for all the plants and trees.

Set in the grounds of the home of the second Lord Harcourt, Nuneham Courtenay was extensively landscaped according to the taste of the period in the early 1780s. It remains a truly wonderful sight, especially in spring, when the blooms seem to fill the air with colour and the trees come into leaf with more variety than one might think imaginable. Bizarrely, the gardens also contain the highly ornate superstructure of the Carfax Conduit, an elaborately carved fountain-head dating from the early seventeenth century, and moved here in 1787, when the Conduit House was demolished.

Fellows Garden
EXETER COLLEGE

A college since Medieval times, Exeter boasts one of the most central positions in Oxford, tucked in between The Broad, Turl Street and the back of the Bodleian. This picture of Exeter's Fellows Garden illustrates beautifully how enclosed most of the Oxford gardens are. Although Exeter's is small by comparison with other colleges, it is nonetheless a haven for the students in the middle of a large city, and contains many beautiful trees. Indeed, in the early eighteenth century, when the Bodleian was seeking to expand westward, the refusal of the Fellows of Exeter to part with any part of their garden resulted in the alteration of the whole scheme, and therefore, indirectly, the construction of the Radcliffe Camera.

The provision of open spaces like gardens was of paramount importance to the late Victorians, including those who redesigned Exeter at that time; they believed passionately in a healthy mind and a healthy body, and it is a typical belief of that period that any college should, out of necessity, have some garden for the benefit of its students.

Gardens
ST JOHN'S COLLEGE

The daffodils and bluebells of St John's garden catch the early spring sunshine, shrouding the view of the east wing of Canterbury Quadrangle and the Laudian Library.

The quadrangle was built between 1631 and 1636, conceived and paid for by William Laud, the Archbishop of Canterbury, Chancellor of the University and a previous President of the College and its Classical grandeur mirrors his position as one of the most important men at the court of Charles I. The garden itself dates back to the foundation of the college as St Bernard's in the fifteenth century, and has been continually altered since then. In 1778, the Fellows' garden and Warden's garden were combined to create a larger space, with a 'grove' to the north, but in 1994 more of the garden was lost with the construction of the new Garden Quadrangle.

The President's garden is now private, open only to Fellows of the College and to the ghosts that are said to haunt its glades.

Fellows' Garden
MERTON COLLEGE

Arguably the oldest of the colleges, Merton was founded in 1264 by Walter de Merton on freehold land at the southern edge of the town. It remains on the edge of the city, with fine views of Christ Church Meadow and the Cherwell to the south, but it nevertheless possesses its own walled garden, the Fellows' Garden, seen here in the mid-afternoon spring sunlight. The fine avenue of trees lead to the east range of Fellows' Quadrangle, one of the earliest parts of the college, and the ancient stone walls are mirrored by the classical herm or 'emperor's head' similar to those which look down on Broad Street outside the Sheldonian Theatre.

The garden is unusual for an Oxford college in that the trees are still a prominent feature; many avenues of trees in other colleges were felled in the Victorian period because of that era's love of lawns, or more specifically, of the game of croquet.

Christ Church Meadow
SOUTH OXFORD

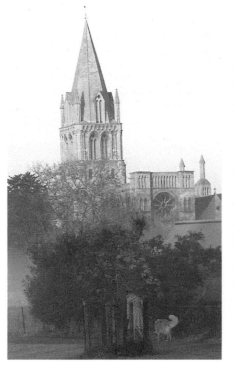

The winter sun barely breaks through the mist to warm the solitary dog-walker on the Broad Walk south of Christ Church College, emphasising the Meadows' proximity to both the Isis and Cherwell. It is down the grand avenue through the Meadows that thousands of spectators make their way to the boat houses for Eights Week every summer; and it is from the balcony of a room in Meadow Quad, seen here, that the 1920s aesthete, Harold Acton read T. S. Eliot's *The Wasteland* to bemused rowers on their way to training, an eccentricity satirised by Evelyn Waugh in *Brideshead Revisited*.

The Meadows have not always been so hospitable: an injunction of the 1860s forbade the entrance of 'all beggars, all persons in dirty clothes, persons of improper character or who are not decent in appearance or behaviour'. Fortunately the Meadows are now open to all; equally fortunately a scheme first suggested in the 1940s to drive a relief road through them to ease traffic congestion has sensibly been scrapped.

The Botanic Garden Gate
EAST OXFORD

The increase in scientific research conducted at the University in the early seventeenth century led to the foundation of the Physic Garden – now the Botanic Garden – on a site to the east of the town near the Cherwell, formerly the Jewish Cemetery. The vision of Henry Danvers, Earl of Danby, it was created in 1621 as a scientific research facility, quite distinct from the recreational gardens that the colleges possessed, and it was Danvers who commissioned the three gateways into the garden through the stone walls. These are modelled on Roman triumphal arches; the main gate, seen here, is especially richly carved, with, unusually, different designs on each side. Its grandeur is such that it is hardly dominated at all by Magdalen Tower immediately behind.

It was not until the late 1940s that a botany school was established in the science area to the north of Oxford; in the preceding centuries all the work done in botanical studies was carried out here, at first in smaller buildings, but after 1835 in an elegant library and lecture room that now forms a part of Magdalen College.

The Botanic Garden

EAST OXFORD

This delightful, walled garden gives a perfect indication of the magnificence of the flora contained in the Botanic Gardens, and in the arboretum six miles out of Oxford at Nuneham Courtenay.

The first gardener of the Physic Garden was Jacob Bobart, a German, who was chosen by Danvers for his extraordinary botanical skills. Described by Anthony Wood as 'an understanding man, the best gardener in England', his memorial tablet remembers him as 'a man of great integrity, chosen by the founder to be keeper of the Physic Garden'. On his death in 1679 his son, Jacob the younger, succeeded him and became Professor of Botany; like his father he became a great Oxford character, not least because of his outlandish appearance, described by von Uffenbach, an ungenerous Oxford visitor of 1710, as 'hideous … and generally villainous'.

The Bobarts' skill in botany and gardening is still alive today in the brilliance of the colours, and above all the heady scents, that are to be found in the modern Botanic Gardens.

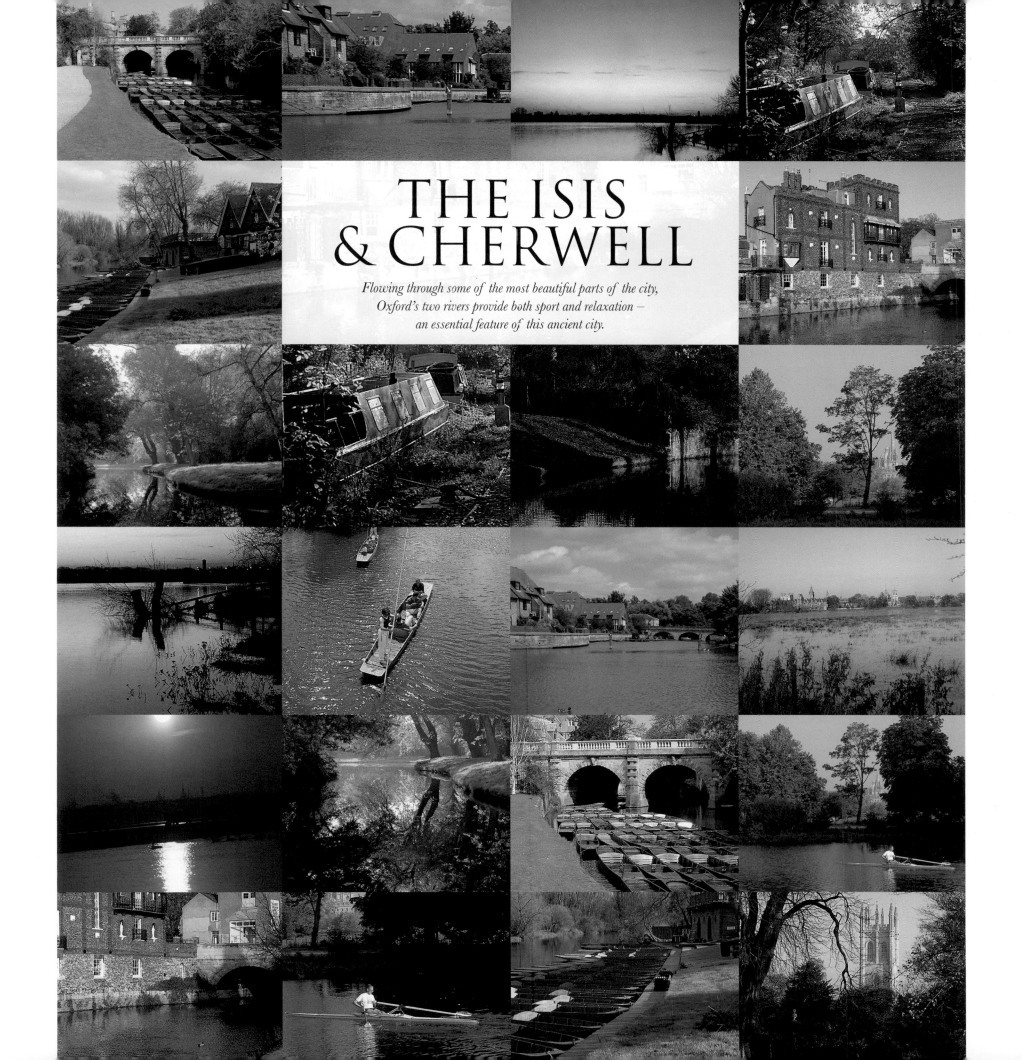

THE ISIS
& CHERWELL

Flowing through some of the most beautiful parts of the city,
Oxford's two rivers provide both sport and relaxation –
an essential feature of this ancient city.

Sculling
THE ISIS

Making the most of the summer sun, a solitary rower sculls past Christ Church Meadows, with St Mary's Church and the Radcliffe Camera in the distance. Not all rowing is done in the coxed eights used in the Boat Race, and this rower is using a fast scull, which look effortlessly simple as they glide swiftly down the river; they are in fact incredibly difficult to balance – and very easy to capsize.

In the nineteenth century rowing was elevated into something approaching religion; in his 1823 *Hints for Oxford*, J. Campbell writes 'In good summer weather the river affords to the sturdy rower an excellent yet cheap amusement. As exercise, there can be nothing in the world better, and we specially advise every reading character to let no fine evening pass without having a good stout pull.' Indeed that most mordant of critics, George Bernard Shaw, noted 'it is characteristic of the authorities at Oxford that they should consider a month too little for the preparation of a boat race, and grudge three weeks to a rehearsal of one of Shakespeare's plays'.

NARROW BOAT
OXFORD & COVENTRY CANAL

Overlooked by Nuffield College spire, a narrow boat lies peacefully alongside the towpath. The Oxford and Coventry Canal lies on the west side of the city, for much of its length actually running alongside the Thames, and the towpath is one of Oxford's most pleasant walks, especially in autumn as the trees turn golden.

The canal was opened in 1790 by the Oxford and Coventry Canal Company, and was enthusiastically promoted by such Oxford luminaries as Sir Roger Newdigate, more famous for instituting the poetry prize which still bears his name. As with other cities across the country, the advent of the canal, as much as the coming of the railway in the next century, changed the nature of Oxford. It encouraged the industrial development of the west side of the city, with its easy access to Coventry and the whole of the newly expanding West Midlands area, and increased Oxford's importance as a trading centre, not merely as an academic one.

Boathouse
THE CHERWELL

The large number of punts lying moored, ready for hire, is evidence of the huge popularity of this sport in Oxford. Most of the colleges have their own punts specifically for the use of their students, kept either here at the Cherwell Boathouse, or by Magdalen or Folly Bridges. The Cherwell is one of the prettiest places to punt in Oxford, as the Isis can become very deep, especially after rain, making it difficult to touch the river bottom, and there is the constant necessity to dodge rowing eights in practise, whose crews have little time for the less-than-adept polesman.

One drawback to punting on the Cherwell used to be an area called Parson's Pleasure, where dons and clergy sunbathed and swam in the nude, and females were required to lie down in the bottom of the punt while they passed, in order to preserve their modesty. However, modern manners have closed Parson's Pleasure, and a lady may now float down the Cherwell unoffended.

PUNTING
THE CHERWELL

The tradition of punting on the rivers at Oxford for pleasure goes back to Victorian times, and is one enthusiastically embraced by most undergraduates today. There are few nicer pastimes than enjoying the peace and tranquillity of gliding so close to the water through the mysterious groves and woods, and out into the fields of North Oxford, seen here.

Originally designed as a means of transporting goods along the shallow rivers, punting is difficult to master at first, and the source of much enjoyment to spectators watching a novice taking his first, uncertain strokes. The pole is pushed into the river bed beneath the boat to propel it forward, and then trailed in the water behind, to act as a rudder in order to steer a course. A muddy stretch of river, or lack of experience, frequently leaves the polesman stranded, clinging to his pole in mid-river, as the punt glides serenely away.

Punts
MAGDALEN BRIDGE

Magdalen Bridge is, for many visitors to Oxford, the first sight they have of the University buildings and the centre of this magical city, standing as it does over the Cherwell on the main road into Oxford from London. It was built between 1772 and 1790, when the old bridge became incapable of carrying the increased coaching traffic, to a design by John Gwynn, a celebrated bridge-builder. With its six arches and elegant Doric columns, it is a masterpiece of Classical architecture and a fitting entrance to the centre of academic Oxford.

In recent years it became the site of some controversy, as the tradition grew among the more excitable undergraduates of adding to the May Morning celebrations which take place around Magdalen Tower, by leaping from the bridge into the Cherwell. This practise was finally stopped by the University authorities when one female undergraduate became front page news in the tabloid newspapers after leaping in entirely unclothed.

The Folly Bridge
THE ISIS

S panning the Thames to the south of the city centre stands Folly Bridge, the main entrance to the city from Abingdon and the south. The current bridge was built between 1825 and 1827, replacing a much older bridge, which dates back to the eleventh century and the aftermath of the Norman Conquest.

Its creator was the Norman knight, Robert d'Oilly, who was responsible for the development of much of Medieval Oxford, most significantly the castle. He had acquired several large estates following the Conquest, and he garrisoned the castle on behalf of King William and as a means of securing his own lands. The first bridge was built under his instruction; called Grandpont, it stood very near the old 'oxen-ford' that gave the city its name. A later addition to the bridge was the defensive tower and gateway, built to guard the entrance to the city, further evidence of the turbulent history that Oxford has witnessed.

The Folly
FOLLY BRIDGE

There have been two follies on Folly Bridge over the centuries since the first building of Grandpont in the eleventh century. The picturesque gateway over the original bridge was called 'Friar Bacon's Study', after the thirteenth-century intellectual, Roger Bacon, a Franciscan Friar and one of Oxford's leading intellectuals of the Middle Ages, a man so ahead of his time that he was accused of practising black magic by his enemies.

This folly was demolished in 1779, and with the construction of its successor beginning in 1825, new buildings grew up around the bridge. These included the stone warehouse that is now the Head of the River public house, and the building seen here, the current 'folly'. Immediately to the south of the bridge, it was built in 1849 by the accountant Joseph Caudwell, a well-known Oxford eccentric. It is largely made of flint, and has a strangely crenellated roof, earning it the nickname 'Caudwell's Castle', although it is now more commonly just referred to as 'the Folly'; another testimony to the generations of eccentrics who add texture to Oxford's rich history.

Sunrise
PORT MEADOW

Just to the north-west of the city centre lies Port Meadow, a vast area of open space, common land for the people of Oxford. This area is mentioned in the Domesday Book of 1086, compiled just after the Norman invasion. It is an area bordered on one side by the Oxford and Coventry canal and on the other by the Thames, which frequently floods in winter – as seen here – to cover the whole low-lying area causing considerable discomfort to the horses that roam freely across the meadow.

Port Meadow is an immensely popular recreational area in Oxford life, and on any fine day you can see kite-flyers; cyclists; walkers just strolling, or heading north to the pretty village of Wolvercote and the Trout Inn; and the inevitable stream of punts along the Thames. It is also an area steeped in history; Charles I rode across it with several hundred horsemen, fleeing the city during the English Civil War. It also has strong literary associations, inspiring many of Oxford's finest writers.

Dawn
PORT MEADOW

As the dawn light breaks over the flooded expanse of Port Meadow, one can see why it has inspired so many writers and poets. Matthew Arnold took his children for walks across the meadow, Kenneth Grahame, author of *The Wind in the Willows*, used to play cricket here, and T. E. Lawrence, 'Lawrence of Arabia', used to canoe across it when it flooded.

Gerard Manley Hopkins, the nineteenth-century poet, wrote one of his best works, *Binsey Poplars* about the felling of the trees that lined its north-western edge:

That dandled a sandalled
Shadow that swam or sank
On meadow and river and wind-wandering weed-
    winding bank.

It was on the part of the Thames bordering the Meadow that Charles Dodgson (Lewis Carroll) first made up the Alice stories in 1862:

All in the golden afternoon,
Full leisurely we glide;
For both our oars, with little skill,
By little arms are plied....
Thus grew the tale of Wonderland:
Thus slowly, one by one,
Its quaint events were hammered out
And now the tale is done,
And home we steer, a merry crew,
Beneath the setting sun.

Magdalen College Tower
THE CHERWELL

Rising majestically above the Cherwell and the autumnal trees, Magdalen Tower stands at the end of Magdalen Bridge as sentinel to Oxford, the first monument of the University to greet the visitor from London. It is one of the most beautiful of all Oxford's sights, a perfect Gothic structure, which had a strong influence on the later Victorian Gothic architecture of Keble College, the Randolph Hotel and other buildings.

Magdalen Tower is the tallest of all the Oxford medieval towers, standing 44 metres (144 feet) high. Its designer is, however, lost in history. The building was begun in 1492, possibly inspired by the designs of the unbuilt tower at King's College, Cambridge, although Merton College Chapel tower has a similar crown of parapets, and there are fifteenth-century churches in Somerset that appear to share an architectural heritage.

As befits its predominant height, it is from the top of this tower that choristers greet the first May morning every year at dawn, marking the beginning of the May Day celebrations.

Floods at Merton
CHRIST CHURCH MEADOW

Rising like an island above the completely flooded Christ Church Meadow, Merton College and the spires of Oxford appear entirely in a world of their own, a cloistered land cut off from the rest of Britain. The climate of the city has been a topic of much congratulation amongst Oxford historians; Anthony Wood wrote of it as 'a place where is a sweet

wholesome and well-tempered aire, such an aire that hath been publickly admired and applauded by persons far and neare', and Daniel Defoe, in his tour through Britain in 1724 remarked that the University is 'so eminent for the goodness of its air and healthy situation, that our courts have no lesse than three times retir'd hither, when London hath been visit'd with the pestilence, and here they have always been safe'.

Although such eulogies seem far-fetched in the middle of an Oxford winter, or when the city is shrouded in the fog that rolls off the rivers, or the Thames seems to be lapping at the very doors of the colleges, there is no doubt that the memory of Oxford in fine weather tends to blot out the recollection of the worse seasons.

River Cherwell
SOUTH OXFORD

The autumn sun catches the trees as their colour turns, the blues and greens reflected in the peaceful Cherwell, and it is easy to see why the rivers of Oxford have proved such fertile inspiration for writers and poets throughout the centuries. As early as the sixteenth century, Edmund Spenser extolled the virtues of the two rivers and the University in his epic poem, *The Faerie Queene*:

that faire city, wherein make abode
So many learned impes, that shoote abroad
And with their branches spread all Britany.
Joy to ye both, ye double nursery
Of Arts, but Oxford thine doth Thame most glorify.

In 1632, the poet John Taylor famously wrote in *The Water-Poet*,

Close under Oxford, one of England's eyes,
Chief of the chiefest Universities,
From Banbury, desirous to add knowledge,
To zeal, and to be taught in Magdalen College,
The River Cherwell doth to Isis runne
And bears her company to Abingdon.

THIS
SPORTING LIFE

*Oxford, like many university towns, has an excellent following in many sports.
All manner of events can be found here, none more popular than rowing,
Oxford's greatest sporting tradition.*

Cricket
WORCESTER COLLEGE

The sound of leather on willow, the immaculate whites, the cries of 'owzat?!', the disdainful shake of the umpire's head; there is nothing more traditionally English than a game of cricket on a sunny afternoon, as the shadow of one of Worcester's beautiful plane trees lengthens across the green turf.

Many of the colleges have their own playing fields, though few are in the position of Worcester in having them in the actual grounds of the college. Thanks to its later development as a college and its position on the fringe of the city centre, Worcester is fortunate in its gardens and playing fields. Most college pitches are further out of town to the north of the city. Cricket is one of Oxford's main summer games, second only to rowing in importance, and there are a series of hotly contested matches between the colleges, as well as matches with other universities.

CRICKET
THE PARKS

Dominated by the imposing form of Keble College Chapel – that monument to Victorian Gothic architecture – a batsman strikes out; the wicket-keeper goes for the catch and another game in England's greatest sporting tradition is under way. Oxford is renowned as a university team, and the very first match of every English county cricket season takes place at the Parks, the Oxford University cricket ground pictured here.

Despite the fact that the start of the season is usually too early for summer to have arrived, and that the game takes place in damp and misty conditions with a very few spectators blowing into their hands in the fading light; despite the fact that the financial burdens of the modern game mean that the University team no longer poses any real threat to the county sides, the tradition remains that the most essentially English of all sports takes its first annual bow on these playing fields.

145

147

College Boat Houses
EIGHTS WEEK

The single most important event in the Oxford sporting calendar is Eights Week, the week when everything else in the University comes to a standstill, and the inhabitants of every college descend on the Isis below Christ Church Meadow to cheer on their teams and barrack the opposition.

Because of the narrowness of the river in many places, it is impossible for two boats to pass, so the races start in an evenly spaced line, with the object of the race being to 'bump' the boat in front. The resulting frenzy is fast and furious, and often rather chaotic, but arouses much passion in the spectators. Thomas Hughes, in *Tom Brown at Oxford* describes the scene: 'the crowds on the bank scatter and rush along, each keeping as near as may be to its own boat. Some of the men on the tow-path, some on the very edge of, often in, the water . . . all at full speed, in wild excitement, and shouting at the top of their voices.'

Rowing at Dawn
THE ISIS

There is no sport in Oxford more important than rowing, and no more committed sportsmen than the rowing eights. Training is usually at dawn, in order to leave the day free for study, although that is frequently replaced by more training in the gym, and the training sessions, often in bitterly cold weather, are ruthlessly demanding. In order to achieve a place in the college first Eight a rower must be fantastically fit and dedicated to his or her sport – for more and more colleges now sport women's teams.

There are, however, advantages in being on the team, and these generally outweigh the hardships; the rowers all dine in Hall on a special protein diet, usually steak, of a much higher culinary level than other students; and in the run up to Eights Week they are excused virtually all academic study. For the winning team, too, the celebrations are boisterous and long-lasting, with the shell of the boats being burned, and champagne and dancing around the fire into the small hours.

Boathouses
THE ISIS

In the first light of a winter dawn, a lone student surveys the river outside the empty boathouses. It is difficult to describe the depth of feeling that rowing inspires in many Oxford students – to achieve the place in a college Eight is a great glory, to achieve a place in the University Eight is beyond all measure.

Thomas Hughes, writing in *Tom Brown at Oxford* in 1861, urges his female readers not to despise this enthusiasm: 'Dear readers of the gentler sex! you, I know, will pardon the enthusiasm which stirs our pulses, now in sober middle age, as we call up again the memories of this the most exciting sport of our boyhood (for we were but boys then, after all...).' The modern sportsman, despite all the intervening years of increased professionalism, American crews and crew mutinies, can still feel the magic of the old Oxford by the river, can still hear the cheers of that more innocent age'.

'THE STREETS WHERE THE GREAT MEN GO'

The streets and pathways of Oxford have been trodden by many a famous figure in their time. A walk through these streets today explains why so many people have been profoundly influenced by this great city.

OXFORD

Holywell Street
EAST OXFORD

Although the present street dates back to the seventeenth century, Holywell Street was an important part of medieval Oxford, and Holywell Manor was one of the ten manors, from as far afield as Surrey, whose livings were appropriated by the founder of Merton College to finance that institution in 1264. The modern street retains much of its seventeenth-century flavour; it is very narrow, especially in comparison to Broad Street, of which it is a continuation, with houses overhanging the road, leading down to the gates of New College and to the edge of medieval Oxford and the city walls.

Many of the houses were built around 1613 to rehouse those inhabitants made homeless by the building of the Examination Schools, and it is a feature of Oxford planning up to this century: that the population has always been considered rather less important than the next phase of University

expansion. Holywell Street is now probably best known for the Holywell Music Room, one of the world's first purpose-built recital rooms.

Cornmarket Street
CENTRAL OXFORD

There is no thoroughfare in Oxford that better demonstrates the city's blend of ancient and modern than Cornmarket Street, for although it is one of the oldest streets in the city, it is also now one of the most aggressively modern.

Cornmarket Street was a part of the earliest Anglo-Saxon settlement, and St Michael's church, seen here, was originally a part of the defensive structure of the eleventh-century town, standing at the north gate, and including in its structure the Bocardo or town jail. At the south of the street was, and still is, Carfax, an intersection of four streets whose name probably derives from the Latin, meaning 'four forks'; this was the market area of Oxford.

The growing importance of the coaching trade meant the destruction of the north gate in 1771, to make way for the wider street that exists today, and the area developed over the years in line with commerce; in 1896 the body of St Martin's church at Carfax was demolished, leaving only the tower that still stands. Now pedestrianised, the Cornmarket is one of Oxford's busiest streets, with modern stores on both sides, jammed with buses down its centre.

The City Centre
MAGDALEN COLLEGE TOWER

Seen here from the top of Magdalen Tower, looking westward across the city to the hills in the distance, Oxford is a city that reflects the diversity of its foundation, and the centuries of growth and change that have made it the modern academic centre and county town that it is today. Seen from above, it shows only the familiar University monuments: the Radcliffe Camera; St Mary's Church; the Examination Schools; Lincoln College Library; with the modern spire of Nuffield College in the distance. On the ground, however, it has amazing diversity in its character, from the broad sweep of St Giles, to the quiet of Merton Lane; from the throbbing traffic of the High Street, to the calm of Radcliffe Square only a stone's throw away.

It is this diversity that gives Oxford its distinct flavour, where every road and every corner holds something of the past, as James Elroy Flecker noted:

Proud and godly kings had built her long ago,
With her towers and tombs and statues all arow,
With her fair and floral air and the love that lingers there,
And the streets where the great men go.

The Castle
WEST OXFORD

On the west side of the city centre, overlooking the river, stands the massive structure of St George's Tower, the only surviving relic of the Norman castle that was built to protect the town of Oxford and the interests of its ruler, Robert d'Oilly, in the late-eleventh century. Now standing in solitary splendour, it was once the tallest of a number of towers which made up the enclosure that was the castle; its superior height and westernmost position standing as a warning of the town's strength to those approaching from the west.

The first accurate map of Oxford, made in 1578 by cartographer Ralph Aga, showed the tower to be clearly still important 500 years later, and also demonstrated its dual role, serving also as the tower of St George's chapel, a church and college of priests founded in 1074, much of which survived in to the eighteenth century. The castle was used in one form or another for many centuries; most notably in 1142 when Empress Matilda was besieged there during the chaotic civil war of Stephen's reign.

The Old City Walls
NEW COLLEGE

Oxford was a thriving town in Anglo-Saxon times, and by the Middle Ages had become one of the most important and largest settlements in the country. The city walls were built in the very early stages of the town's history, but were rebuilt completely in the years 1226 and 1240, not only to keep enemies out and protect the town through the frequent civil wars of the period, but also as a mark of the town's importance and sense of civic pride.

Judging from these relics in the gardens of New College, they were an impressive achievement: with a raised walkway, bastions with arrow-slits and an outer defence wall to the north. Four main gates allowed access to the city, one on each side, with other smaller gates at intervals; these have all now disappeared, the main gates to the south and west being demolished in the early seventeenth century, the north and east in 1771 to allow better access to the city for the coaching trade.

Museum of Oxford
ST ALDATES

Tucked in a narrow alley off St Aldate's, to the south of the city centre, stands the Museum of Oxford, the city's own museum about Oxford's history and past, offering an insight into the growth of the town of Oxford, rather than the University.

It is an essential part of the city's character that it has grown up alongside the University, retaining its role as a county town, not surrendering wholly to the academics who brought it its fame; the history of 'town and gown' has not always been a happy one. As early as 1298 records tell of a fracas between the town officials and 'some clerks of the University who came to fight and disturb the peace . . . whereupon hue and cry was raised', and in 1354 the battle of St Scholastica took place – its cause some bad wine – in which students and citizens skirmished for some days, with a resultant loss of life on both sides. The city was blamed for the upset, and for the next 500 years had to pay a fine to the University.

Little Clarendon Street
NORTH OXFORD

Running between St Giles and Walton Street, Little Clarendon Street marks the end of University Oxford and the beginning of North Oxford, and has a character all its own. Nicknamed 'Little Trendy Street' it gained fame in the 1970s and 1980s as the street in Oxford with the most fashionable restaurants, bars and shops within its short distance, a street which had some of the cosmopolitan flavour of London lacking in most other parts of the city.

The relative affluence of undergraduates at that time prompted an explosion of consumer outlets aimed at them, although the last 15 years have seen that affluence seriously eroded. Nevertheless, Oxford has retained its more fashionable, less provincial, status, and has partly thrown off the fusty academic atmosphere it had until the 1950s, not least through a series of urban redevelopment schemes at the very heart of the city centre.

Jericho
NORTH-WEST OXFORD

As the visitor to Oxford heads north from Worcester College, passing the new Oxford University Press building, the character of the city changes dramatically, as the roads become more suburban, the houses smaller and terraced, and the monumental grandeur is left far behind. This is Jericho, an area developed in the eighteenth and nineteenth centuries as the population of Oxford began to rise, with the increased trade first brought about by the growing coaching trade, then with the arrival of the canal and the railway.

The name 'Jericho' is of very uncertain provenance, although there are many different theories. One suggests that it derives from the legend above a local pub 'Tarry ye at Jericho'; another that it was because the area housed a large number of Oxford's Jewish population – there is still a synagogue in Richmond Road; still another that the whistles of the trains roaring past the western fringe of the area could make the walls tumble down. Whatever the reason for the name, this area remains distinctly separate from the rest of the city.

St Barnabas Church
JERICHO

The rising working-class population of Oxford in the nineteenth century, thanks in no small measure to the arrival of the canal and railway, meant that areas like Jericho, close to both, developed rapidly to accommodate them. As the building works gathered pace, so did the religious missions eager to save the souls of the new parishioners and the relaxation of Oxford's stringent conformity laws meant that other religious persuasions were free to develop in the city.

Seen here across the canal basin, St Barnabas was built between 1869 and 1872 as an Anglo-Catholic mission to the new working-class inhabitants. It was founded by Thomas Combe, a wealthy High Churchman, follower of the Oxford Movement, and Printer to the University, and it is noticeable that the design is very simple, without any of the Victorian-Gothic extravagances that were the fashion of the time. Its Italianate tower is fitting to a creed which sought to bring closer the beliefs of Canterbury and Rome.

ENTERTAINMENT

Oxford boasts its fair share of leisure opportunities: from cinemas to many well-known pubs that have been the watering holes of generations of famous students, providing an escape from the pressures of academic life.

The Oxford Playhouse
BEAUMONT STREET

Many of British theatre's most successful actors have started their careers at Oxford, and most have played at the Playhouse, situated in Beaumont Street. It is a relatively small theatre, built in 1938, but has played host to many major stars, and is used by professional companies as well as by the students.

Drama at Oxford is not taught as a course, but thousands of students spend much of their time immersed in theatre; there are many college drama societies, and the Oxford University Dramatic Society (OUDS) is world famous. In any week during term, the visitor is spoiled for choice of theatrical experience.

Among the actors who have started their careers here are Rowan Atkinson, Dudley Moore, Michael Palin, Robert Hardy, Hugh Grant and most notably perhaps, Richard Burton. Burton came to Exeter College in 1944 and gained a reputation as a great performer while at Oxford. In 1966 he returned with Elizabeth Taylor to perform in *Dr Faustus*, raising the money to build the studio theatre of the Playhouse: the Burton-Taylor rooms.

Holywell Music Room
HOLYWELL STREET

Built in 1780, the Holywell Music Room, for all its lack of pretension, is one of the premier concert rooms in the country, and was one of the very first purpose-built auditoria for the public presentation of music. Although it has the appearance of a Non-Conformist chapel, it boasts a rich musical heritage: Haydn conducted rehearsals in this room, and wrote his 'Oxford' Symphony to celebrate being awarded an honorary degree by the University.

Oxford has an impressive musical tradition, and many great composers and performers have studied here: Thomas Beecham was at Wadham College, although he left without taking a degree; William Walton was a chorister at the Cathedral Choir School, and later an undergraduate; Ivor Novello was a chorister at Magdalen; and Oscar-winning composer Rachel Portman was at Worcester. Perhaps most famously, George Frederick Handel promoted and conducted at his own Oxford Festival in 1773, introducing the organ concerto to Britain, and reaffirming Oxford's importance in the world of music.

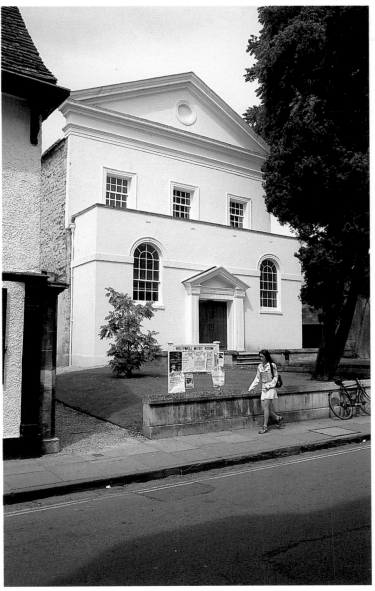

Brown's Restaurant
ST GILES

One of the most popular restaurants in Oxford, Brown's has spawned a whole chain of eating establishments throughout Britain. It is a great favourite with students, and long queues frequently form at weekends, with undergraduates eager to escape the food in college.

Despite the opulence of many of the college dining halls, the food frequently leaves much to be desired and many students prefer to eat out of college. The formality of much college dining is also a deterrent: many colleges insist a tie and gown be worn for dinner; also a great number of students live in rented accommodation (digs) rather than in college. Increased grants to students in the 1970s and 1980s meant that most were more affluent, and therefore able to eat better. This has meant a huge rise in the number of restaurants in Oxford, catering to the student population, offering a large variety of cuisines; of them all Brown's has established itself as an Oxford tradition, featuring prominently in the Oxford film, *Privileged*.

The Ultimate Picture Palace
EAST OXFORD

The successor to an Oxford student legend, the Penultimate Picture Palace, or PPP as it was known to generations of students, the Ultimate Picture Palace is one of Oxford's best art-house cinemas. At a time when the larger cinemas are increasingly a part of the giant film companies, showing only the latest American blockbusters, it provides a lifeline to students interested in cinema and the developments in film in Europe and the Far East, as well as providing the opportunity to see the greatest movies of the past.

Since its inception at the beginning of the century, Oxford has proved a rich inspiration for film, as well as educating many of its leading exponents. From early films, such as *A Yank at Oxford*, through to modern movies like *Privileged* and *Shadowlands*, the magic of Oxford has delighted film makers; and modern directors John Schlesinger, Michael Hoffman, Nicholas Hytner and Michael Caton Jones all studied here, as did actors Hugh Grant, Kris Kristofferson, Sam West and the late Richard Burton.

St Giles Fair
ST GILES

Life at the University is not all academic drudgery, and every autumn, the street of St Giles comes alive with the excitement of the travelling fair. Although the rides and stalls are all modern, the tradition of these travelling fairs dates back to medieval times. Known often as 'mop' fairs, they were frequently the only form of entertainment on offer in an otherwise gruelling existence, with jugglers, acrobats and performers of all kinds, although they were thought by many to be iniquitous and the devil's work.

In 1636 William Laud, Chancellor of the University, included in his code of rules for undergraduates: 'Neither rope dancers nor players, nor sword matches, or sword players are to be permitted within the University of Oxford. All stage players, rope dancers and fencers transgressing are to be incarcerated.' The rules of the University today fortunately make it possible to enjoy a night on the big wheel and the dodgems without fear of arrest.

MORRIS DANCING
BROAD STREET

Morris dancers celebrate the beginning of May in traditional style on Broad Street, outside the Clarendon Building and Hertford College. Morris dancing is an old British custom that almost died out in the late-nineteenth century, but has since experienced something of a revival, and is now a very popular pastime for many people. It dates back to the medieval period, and was a part of the Feast of Fools that Shakespeare wrote of in *Twelfth Night*, celebrating the richness of the countryside and the harvest to come.

The celebration of May Morning is an old Oxford tradition, and is most notable for the dawn salute to the rising sun given by choristers from Magdalen College School atop Magdalen Tower, described here by Oona Howard Ball at the turn of this century: 'the coming out into the morning mists, the burst of song just as the sun rises, the clashing of the glorious Magdalen bells which seem to sway the slender tower. Then caps and gowns are thrown wildly in the air . . . then off to the meadows.'

The Bear
BEAR LANE

One of the prettiest and most popular of Oxford's many pubs, the Bear is also unquestionably the smallest. Tucked in to a corner behind Christ Church, it is thought to date back to 1242 and to derive its name from its position over an old bear-baiting pit, one of medieval England's least-attractive sports, which thrived right up to the age of Shakespeare and beyond. Among the oddities of this tavern is that it is built entirely without any right angles internally – although it is frequently so crowded that it is hard even to see the walls – and that the bar is made entirely of pewter.

The Bear also boasts two resident ghosts, one a landlord who shot himself in the cellar, 'he couldn't hang himself as the cellar is only two foot high'; and it also contains an extraordinary collection of ties, nearly 5,000 of them, all mounted behind glass on the walls.

Head Of The River
THE ISIS

To sit in the sun outside this recently converted public house and watch the swans swim gracefully by, and students punting along the Isis, is to see Oxford at its most leisurely. The building itself has a history of industry, dating back to the days when the river traded in goods, not people, and one can still see relics of its days as a loading warehouse.

Oxford boasts so many public houses that it is difficult to remember that such places were not always smiled upon; in his Code of 1636, Archbishop Laud decreed 'it is enacted that scholars of all conditions shall keep away from inns, eating houses and wine shops within the City wherein wine or any other drink, or the Nicotian herb or tobacco is commonly sold, and if any person does otherwise and is . . . not a graduate, he shall be flogged in public.' The popular history of the University suggests, however, that Laud's strictures were widely and enthusiastically ignored.

The Eagle and Child
ST GILES

One of Oxford's most notable pubs, the Eagle and Child has many historical and literary associations dating back to before the English Civil War. During that conflict it was used as a payhouse for the Royalist army, and up until the late-eighteenth century, pony auctions were held in the back yard, which was also used as a dairy.

However, it was in the 1940s that the 'Bird and Baby' gained its main fame as the drinking haunt of the writers C. S. Lewis, his brother William, J. R. R. Tolkien and Christopher Williams, or 'the Inklings' as they used to refer to themselves. The Rabbit room in the inn rang to stories about Narnia and Hobbits, and Tolkien wrote in a letter to Lewis, 'I know no more pleasant sound than arriving at the "B and B" and hearing a roar, and knowing that one can plunge in.'

One further idiosyncrasy: the rubber pavement outside the pub is not for the safety of over-indulgent visitors, but to stop the flagstones breaking when barrels are dropped on them.

Bicycles
PARKS ROAD

The lamps go on outside the King's Arms pub and a crowd of students gather in the street to drink, to talk over the day's events, or to plan the entertainment for the evening ahead. In front of them, in serried ranks, bicycles stand ready to transport them wherever they wish to go.

One of the most familiar sights of Oxford since the nineteenth century has been the bike, which is the main mode of transport in the city; the crowded streets make driving a nightmare, but the advent of colleges further afield from the very centre of the city make some form of transport a necessity.

Wherever one goes in Oxford the bicycle rules supreme, and there is good provision for them, with racks throughout the town, and cycle lanes, although here the green traffic light for cyclists is rendered useless by the crowd of drinkers blocking it. The most extraordinary sight is the hundreds of bikes locked outside the railway station, a veritable elephant's graveyard of the bicycle.

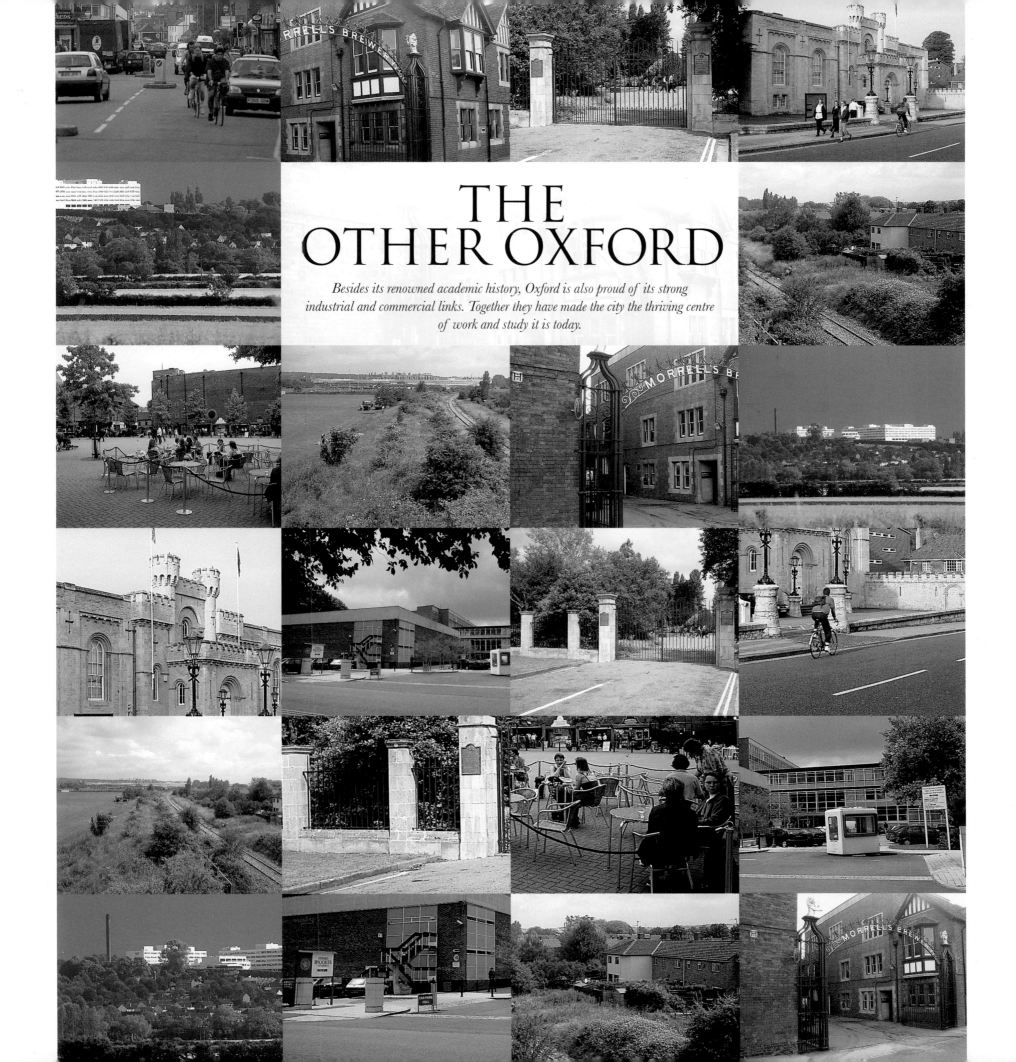

THE OTHER OXFORD

Besides its renowned academic history, Oxford is also proud of its strong industrial and commercial links. Together they have made the city the thriving centre of work and study it is today.

Cowley Road
EAST OXFORD

The magic and mystery of Oxford, the cloisters, the rivers, the hushed recesses of the Bodleian, fade as the visitor leaves the centre of the city, and discovers the 'other Oxford': the industrial and commercial part of the city which grew up around the University and expanded enormously in the middle of this century. Watched over by the distant spire of St Mary's, the Cowley Road is at the very heart of this nonetheless integral part of the city, albeit a part that is a source of endless amusement to undergraduates of Cambridge, who never fail to mention Oxford's car factories.

It is largely due to one man, William Morris, later Lord Nuffield, that the motor industry came to Oxford. From humble beginnings in a bicycle repair shop, he graduated to cars, and by 1913 he had established in Cowley his first factory, producing 30 cars a week with a staff of 12. With the enormous growth in the motor industry between the wars, Cowley became one of the largest car producers in the country, employing more than 10,000 people by 1926, a vast workforce that required housing and services near to the factories.

Florence Park
COWLEY

The grand gates and tree-lined avenues of Florence Park suggest that the visitor is about to experience commercial Oxford's version of the Botanic gardens, but in fact this park is another result of the motor industry's invasion of the city. Designed by F. E. Moss and built between 1933 and 1937, it contains a vast housing estate, designed for letting accommodation to car workers who could not afford to buy their own homes.

Over 5,000 new homes were built in Oxford during the 1930s, and many of these were of very low standards, little better than slum dwellings. At Florence Park, however, Moss attempted to break the depressing monotony of the housing estates. He placed the houses alongside a large, green park, which was opened in 1936 – the gates of which can be seen here – and made the approach to the housing area a wide, tree-lined avenue, with shops for the convenience of the workers' wives, a munificence rare for that depressed era, and in sharp contrast to other estates of the same period.

Blackbird Leys Estate
COWLEY

Blackbird Leys is a prime example of the more modern housing estates that give present-day Oxford its dual identity: academic and commercial; with the Cowley car works in the background, and bordered by the railway that played so important a part in Oxford's industrial expansion. The estate was begun in 1957 by the town council and expanded greatly in 1966, when the population of St Ebbe's in the city were moved here, many unwillingly.

The division between the two Oxfords has not always been a happy one, and there have always been those who despaired of the industrial giant growing on the outskirts; from the Architectural Review of 1929: 'Oxford today has little claim to be regarded as better than the rest of our semi-manufacturing, semi-commercial slums . . . it would be ridiculous for those who have eyes to pretend that Oxford as a town today is greatly superior to Croydon.' Although we may choose to agree with Clare, the heroine of Galsworthy's *The End of a Chapter*, looking at the University centre: 'Whatever they do to the outside, I don't see how they can spoil all this.'

John Radcliffe Hospital
HEADINGTON

Rising bold and stark above the east Oxford skyline, John Radcliffe Hospital's sheer size pays eloquent testimony to the city's increased population, and its importance as a county town as well as an academic centre. The construction of the new hospital began in 1968, when it had become abundantly clear that the older institutions had become hopelessly outdated.

Chief of these was the old Radcliffe Infirmary, built to the north of the city on the Woodstock Road between 1759 and 1767 on land donated by Thomas Rowney, one of the city's Members of Parliament. The original was a grand building, built in an English Palladian style, reflecting the increasing ambition of the University's founders, as well as their increasing knowledge of medicine. As the city expanded so too did the need for space, and the building was altered according to that need, with a large extension added in 1911, and more in the following decades, eventually swamping the original eighteenth-century building. By the early 1960s it became clear a fresh start was needed.

Oxford County Hall
NEW ROAD

Oxford is not merely an academic institution, but also the administrative centre for the whole county of Oxfordshire; and the County Hall in New Road was built in 1839 to house the assize courts that had outgrown their previous home in the Town Hall. A Neo-Norman building, it emphasises the city's historical origins; the building is positioned within the precincts of the original castle.

Fittingly for an assize court, the County Hall is sited next to the Oxford County jail. As one would expect from a city with such a turbulent past, the history of the jail has been varied; originally situated over the North Gate of the city, and dating back to the eleventh century, the 'Bocardo' as it was known, was demolished in 1771, to be replaced with a new town jail on Gloucester Green, in 1789. This in turn only lasted until 1878, by which time the present county jail, begun in 1785, became the central jail for both city and county. A grim building, its most notable feature is the execution platform, a tower where public executions were held up until 1863.

Brookes University
HEADINGTON

Nowhere illustrates more vividly the existence of another Oxford than Brookes University, situated east of the city in Headington, just before the hill that takes the visitor down into the city centre. Founded in the early 1950s by the city council, and known then as Oxford Polytechnic, it was established as a rival to the University, to counter the perceived elitism and snobbery of that institution, with its vast preponderance of public school students from wealthy backgrounds.

It was immediately successful, and in the early 1990s was granted university status in the opening up of the educational system throughout Britain; it is now a firmly established alternative to the university down the hill. Its administrative centre is now in Headington Hall, lately the home of the publisher, Robert Maxwell; and in one of Oxford's nicer ironies, its featureless curtain-walled buildings, so typical of the 1960s, house Oxford's only school of architecture.

Oxford Past and Present

This map shows a bird's eye view of Oxford as it was in the sixteenth century. The original version of the map was drawn up in 1578 by the cartographer Ralph Agas (c. 1540–1621) and was the first accurate map of the city. This reduced sized engraving of the map was created in 1823 by Joseph Skelton, an Oxford man.

The map emphasises Oxford's ancient academic tradition – a number of the colleges can be seen here with their grounds, meadows and orchards. Amongst those standing at the time were: Magdalen College (Magdalaine Colledge); New College (Sainte Marias Colledge alias Newe Colledge); Queen's College (Quenes Colledge); Lincoln College (Earl of Linc); Christ Church College (Chrystes Churtch Colledge); Jesus College (Jhesus Colledge); Exeter College (Exeter Colledge); Corpus Christi College (Corp Chris); St John's College (St John's Colledge); Trinity College (Trinity Colledge); Balliol College (Baliol Colledge); All Souls College (All Souls Colledge); and Merton College (Merton Colledge).

Other features of the sixteenth-century city are still evident today: Christ Church Meadow (Christes Churtch Meadowes and Walkes) to the south; the church of St Giles standing way out beyond the northern boundaries of the city here; the street that is now St Giles leading up to bisect with the High Street (Highe Streate) which runs through the centre of the city from the East Gate; the familiar branches of the Cherwell (River Charwell) under the East Bridge (now Magdalen Bridge). Other features of the city have disappeared, most notably the castle prison (Castell Prison) in the west. Built to protect the city in Norman times, the map shows large parts of the castle still standing and still playing an important role. The only part of this that remains is St George's Tower.

North Oxford
14, 18, 21, 25, 30, 31, 32, 36, 64, 65, 70, 72, 75, 76, 77, 79, 82, 87, 113, 114, 130, 132, 136, 137, 145, 157, 167, 168, 169, 172, 174, 176, 180, 182, 184

East Oxford
73, 86, 111, 112, 124, 125, 133, 138, 188, 189, 190, 191, 195

South Oxford
15, 25, 29, 56, 58, 69, 98, 99, 119, 123, 128, 134, 135, 139, 140, 148, 150, 151, 166, 178, 179

West Oxford
33, 80, 89, 110, 129, 144, 146, 164, 175, 192, 193, 194

Central Oxford
16, 19, 20, 24, 26, 34, 35, 37, 38, 39, 40, 42, 43, 44, 46, 47, 48, 49, 50, 51, 54, 56, 59, 60, 61, 62, 63, 66, 67, 68, 74, 78, 81, 83, 84, 88, 90, 91, 94, 95, 96, 100, 101, 102, 103, 104, 105, 106, 107, 116, 117, 118, 120, 121, 122, 147, 154, 155, 156, 158, 159, 160, 162, 163, 165, 173, 179, 183, 185

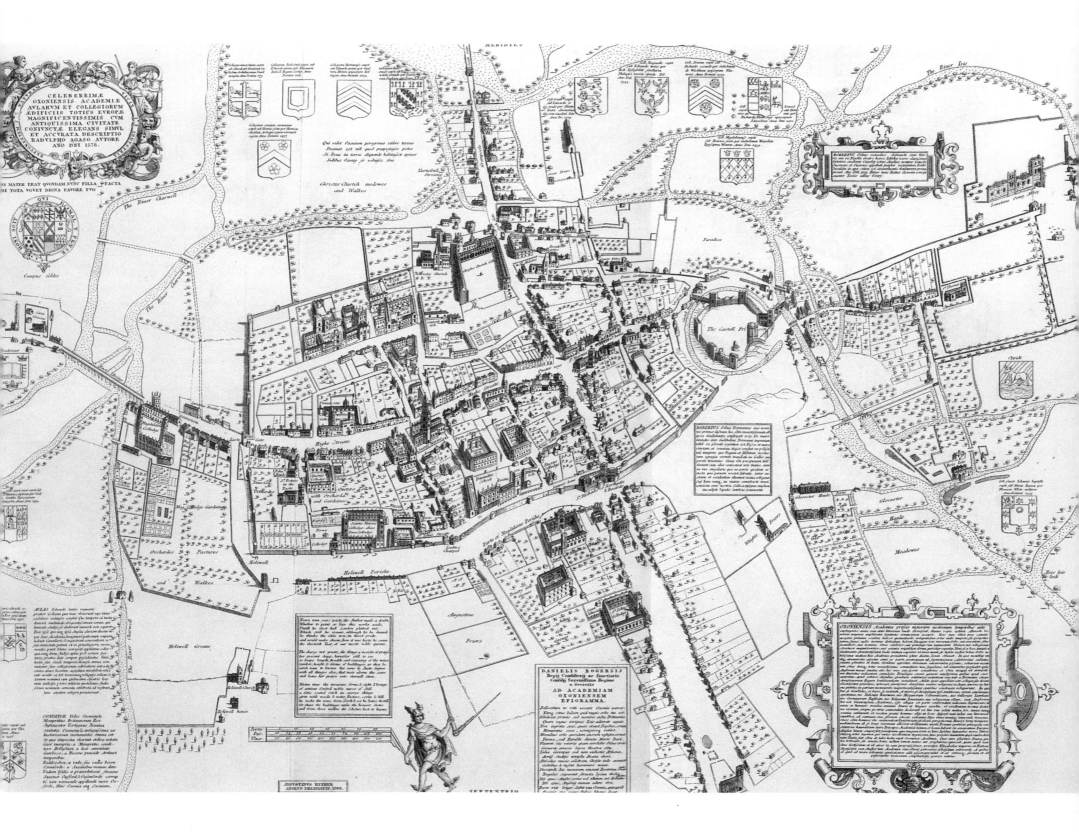

Index